# A Simple Guide to Using the
# SΛMSUNG Galaxy Tab S7 & S7+

A Simple Guide to Using the

# SAMSUNG
## Galaxy Tab S7 & S7+

A Simplified User Manual for Beginners — with Useful Tips and Tricks

Dylan Blake & Patrick Garner

While every precaution has been taken in preparing this book, the publisher does not claim any liability for mistakes or omissions, or damages arising from the use of the information contained herein.

**A Simple Guide to Using the Samsung Galaxy Tab S7 & S7+**

**First edition. November 6th, 2020.**

ISBN: 9798563684768

Copyright © 2020 Dylan Blake

Written by Dylan Blake and Patrick Garner

# Contents

INTRODUCTION ................................................................. i

1: Getting Started ............................................................. 1

Unboxing the Galaxy Tab S7 and S7+ .......................... 4

Power on Your Device ..................................................... 5

Setting up Your Galaxy Tab S7 and S7+ ...................... 6

Transfer Data from Your Old Devices ........................... 8

    Transferring Data via USB Cable ............................. 8

    Transferring Data via Wi-Fi .................................... 10

Lock and Unlock Your Device ..................................... 12

    Types of Screen Lock ............................................... 12

    Securing Your Device with Screen Lock ............... 13

Biometric Security ......................................................... 18

    Face Recognition ..................................................... 19

    Managing Face Recognition .................................. 19

    Using Fingerprint ..................................................... 21

    Managing Fingerprint ............................................ 21

    Biometrics Preferences ........................................... 23

Remapping the Side Key Function ............................. 24

Customize the Home Screen ............................................... 27

    App Icons ........................................................................ 27

    How to Create and Use Folders ................................... 28

    Wallpaper ....................................................................... 28

    Themes ........................................................................... 29

    Widget ............................................................................ 30

    Home screen settings ................................................... 31

    Status Bar ...................................................................... 33

    Notification Panel ........................................................ 35

    Quick settings ............................................................... 36

## 2: The S Pen – Samsung's Magic Wand .................... 39

Air Actions ............................................................................ 40

    Press and hold shortcut .............................................. 41

    Anywhere actions ........................................................ 41

    App actions .................................................................. 42

    General app actions .................................................... 43

Air View ................................................................................ 43

Air Command ...................................................................... 44

    Create notes .................................................................. 46

    View all notes ............................................................... 46

Smart select ............................................................. 46

Screen write ............................................................ 47

Live messages ......................................................... 48

AR Doodle ............................................................... 49

Translate ................................................................. 50

PENUP ...................................................................... 51

Add shortcuts .......................................................... 51

Screen off Memo ......................................................... 52

Pin to Always on Display ....................................... 52

Configure S Pen Settings ............................................ 53

Air command ......................................................... 54

Removal ................................................................. 54

Feedback ................................................................ 54

General ................................................................... 55

Replace the S Pen tip or nib ....................................... 55

## 3: Using Apps ............................................................ 57

Download Apps ........................................................... 57

Disable or Uninstall Apps ........................................... 57

Search for Apps ............................................................ 58

Sort Apps ....................................................................... 58

Create a New Folder ............................................................. 59

    Moving folder to my home screen ............................... 59

    Deleting a folder .......................................................... 60

Game Booster ....................................................................... 60

    Using the pop-up panel ................................................ 61

App settings ......................................................................... 62

## 4: Samsung Apps .............................................................. 65

Galaxy Essentials .................................................................. 65

Bixby ..................................................................................... 66

AR Zone ................................................................................ 66

Galaxy Store ......................................................................... 66

Game Launcher .................................................................... 67

PENUP .................................................................................. 67

Samsung Members .............................................................. 67

SmartThings ......................................................................... 68

Tips ....................................................................................... 68

Calculator ............................................................................. 69

Calendar ............................................................................... 69

    Add Calendars .............................................................. 70

    Subscription Calendars ................................................ 70

Calendar Alert Styles ... 71

Create an Event ... 71

Delete an Event ... 71

Clock ... 72

Alarm ... 72

Delete an Alarm ... 73

World clock ... 73

Time Zone Converter ... 74

Weather Settings ... 75

Stopwatch ... 75

Timer ... 75

Preset Timer ... 76

Timer Options ... 76

General settings ... 77

Contacts ... 77

Edit a Contact ... 78

Call or Message a Contact ... 78

Favorites ... 78

Share a Contact ... 79

Direct Share ... 79

- Groups .................................................................. 79
- Manage Contacts ................................................. 81
- Internet ..................................................................... 83
  - Browser Tabs ........................................................ 84
  - Bookmarks ............................................................ 84
  - Open a Bookmark ................................................ 84
  - Save a Web Page ................................................. 84
  - View History ........................................................ 84
  - Share Pages .......................................................... 85
  - Secret Mode ......................................................... 85
  - Internet Settings .................................................. 86
- Messages ................................................................... 86
  - Message Search .................................................... 86
  - Delete Conversations .......................................... 87
  - Emergency Alerts ................................................ 87
  - Send SOS Messages ............................................ 87
  - Message Settings ................................................. 88
- My Files .................................................................... 88
  - File Groups ........................................................... 89
  - My Files Options ................................................. 89

Phone ................................................................................. 90

    Calls ............................................................................. 91

    Making a Phone call ................................................. 91

    Using swipes to call ................................................. 91

    Making a call from Recent ..................................... 91

    Making a call from contact .................................... 91

    Answer a call ............................................................. 92

    Decline a call ............................................................. 92

    Decline with a message .......................................... 92

    End a call ................................................................... 93

    Actions while on a call ............................................ 93

    Multitask .................................................................... 93

    Switch to speakers or headsets ............................ 93

    Call pop-up settings ................................................ 94

    Manage calls ............................................................. 94

    Voicemail .................................................................... 97

    Phone settings .......................................................... 97

    Optional calling services ........................................ 98

    Video calls ................................................................. 98

    Place a multiparty call ............................................ 98

Wi-Fi calling..................................................................99

Samsung notes ...........................................................99

    Create notes ........................................................ 100

    Voice recordings ................................................. 100

    Edit notes ............................................................ 100

    Note options ......................................................102

    Notes menu .......................................................102

Samsung Flow ..........................................................103

**5: The Bixby** .............................................................**105**

What Is Bixby?..........................................................105

Getting Started with Bixby................................... 106

Changing Bixby Settings.......................................107

Bixby Home...............................................................107

Bixby Voice: Blabbing with Bixby ....................... 109

Bixby Vision .............................................................. 111

Bixby Routines ........................................................ 112

**6: Camera**..................................................................**115**

Using the Galaxy Tab S7 Cameras ...................... 116

Navigating the Camera Screen............................ 116

Configuring Your Shooting Mode....................... 117

Other shooting modes ................................................. 118

AR Zone ................................................................. 118

Single Take ............................................................ 119

Live Focus ............................................................. 120

Scene Optimizer ..................................................... 120

Recording Videos ................................................... 120

Live Focus Video .................................................... 121

Camera Settings ............................................................ 121

Intelligent Features ................................................ 122

Pictures ................................................................. 122

Video .................................................................... 123

Useful Features ............................................................ 123

**7: Gallery** ................................................................ 127

View pictures ............................................................... 128

Edit pictures ................................................................ 129

View videos ................................................................. 130

Video enhancer ............................................................ 131

Edit videos .................................................................. 131

Share pictures and videos ............................................. 132

Delete pictures and videos ............................................ 132

Create a movie .................................................. 133

Take a Screenshot .............................................. 134

    Use Palm Swipe to Capture a Screenshot ............... 134

    Screenshot Settings ..................................... 134

Screen Recorder ................................................ 135

    Screen Recorder Settings ................................ 135

## 8: Display ................................................ 137

Motion Smoothness ............................................ 138

Screen Resolution ............................................. 138

Dark Mode .................................................... 139

Screen Brightness ............................................. 140

Blue Light Filter .............................................. 140

Screen Mode .................................................. 141

Font Size and Style ........................................... 141

Screen Zoom .................................................. 142

Screen Timeout ............................................... 142

Accidental Touch Protection .................................. 143

Show Charging Information ................................... 143

Screen Saver .................................................. 143

Reduce Animations ............................................ 144

Double-tap to Wake .................................................................. 144

Smart Stay .................................................................................. 145

## 9: Connections ................................................................. 147

Wi-Fi ........................................................................................... 147

    Manually connect to a Wi-Fi network ....................... 148

    Advanced Wi-Fi settings ................................................ 149

    Wi-Fi Direct ....................................................................... 150

    Disconnect from Wi-Fi Direct ...................................... 151

Bluetooth ................................................................................. 151

    Renaming a Paired Device ........................................... 152

    Unpair from a Bluetooth Device ................................. 152

    Advanced Options .......................................................... 152

    Dual Audio ........................................................................ 153

Airplane Mode ........................................................................ 154

Mobile networks .................................................................... 154

Data Usage ............................................................................... 155

    Turn on Data Saver ......................................................... 155

    Monitor Mobile Data ..................................................... 155

    Monitor Wi-Fi Data ........................................................ 156

Mobile Hotspot ...................................................................... 157

Change the Mobile Hotspot Password ................... 157

Configuring the Mobile Hotspot Settings ................ 157

Wi-Fi Sharing ................................................................. 159

Band .............................................................................. 159

Auto Hotspot ................................................................ 159

Tethering ............................................................................ 159

Nearby Device Scanning .................................................. 160

Connect to a Printer ......................................................... 160

Virtual Private Networks .................................................. 161

Managing a VPN .......................................................... 161

Connecting to a VPN ................................................... 162

Private DNS ........................................................................ 162

Ethernet .............................................................................. 162

**10: Other Cool Features ............................................. 165**

Samsung DeX ..................................................................... 165

Microsoft apps ................................................................... 168

Outlook ......................................................................... 168

LinkedIn ........................................................................ 168

Office ............................................................................ 168

OneDrive ...................................................................... 168

Edge screen ................................................................. 168

    Configure Edge panels ................................................ 169

    Edge panel position ..................................................... 170

    Edge panel style ............................................................ 171

    Apps panel .................................................................... 171

Multi Window .............................................................. 172

    Window Controls ........................................................ 173

xCloud- Xbox game streaming ......................................... 174

**About the Author** ...................................................... **175**

**Index** ............................................................................ **177**

# INTRODUCTION

Congratulations on purchasing the latest member of the Samsung Galaxy tab series. Now that you have this beauty, it's time to put to good use all it has to offer by making use of a well-illustrated user manual that unlocks all its hidden tips and tricks. This user guide has been specially constructed to give you precisely what you need, with so many tips and tricks to help you become familiar with the Samsung Galaxy Tab S7 and S7+.

The Samsung Galaxy Tab S7 and S7+ come with many similar features as the Samsung flagship phones made in 2020, that is, the S20, S20 Ultra, Note20, and Note20 Ultra devices. A clear-cut example is the 120Hz refresh rate. You get to choose between 60Hz and 120Hz – that is, there is no adaptive frequency screen. Nonetheless, when a high-frequency rate isn't needed, your device screen will return to 60Hz. For example, when streaming a video or using apps that don't support high refresh rates, your tablet drops automatically to 60Hz.

Another key feature is the S pen, which has been improved from a latency of 45ms down to 9ms – just like the Note20 and Note20 Ultra. This Device also comes with the Qualcomm Snapdragon 865+ processor, which undoubtedly contributed to the overall enhancement of the S pen. We'll be uncovering more functionalities and hidden features of this Device as we proceed further in this simplified user manual.

There are so many features to explore in your new Samsung Galaxy Device. And to get you started, we'll have to begin with the basics, so we don't leave anything untouched or any stone unturned. Let's get started!

# 1

# Getting Started

Before we can proceed into more advanced ways to operate and manage your new Device, let's look at the layouts of the S7 and S7+ Samsung Galaxy Tabs. If what you're holding in your hand doesn't look like one of these devices, as shown below, then there is a high chance that you got something else.

2    A Simple Guide to Using the Samsung Galaxy Tab S7 & S7+

## The Samsung Galaxy Tab S7

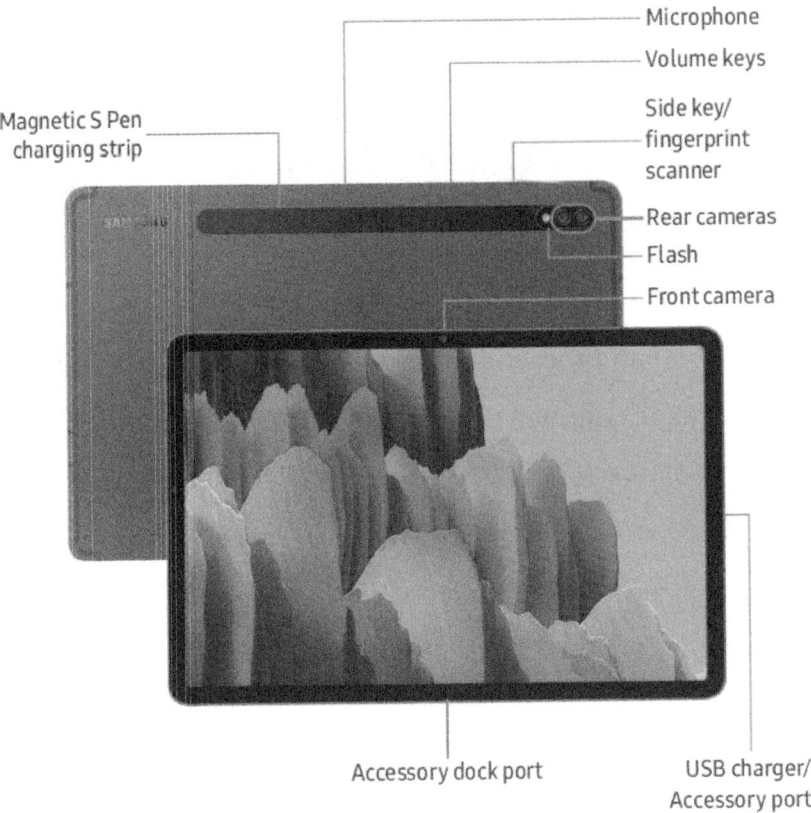

1: Getting Started 3

# The Samsung Galaxy Tab S7+

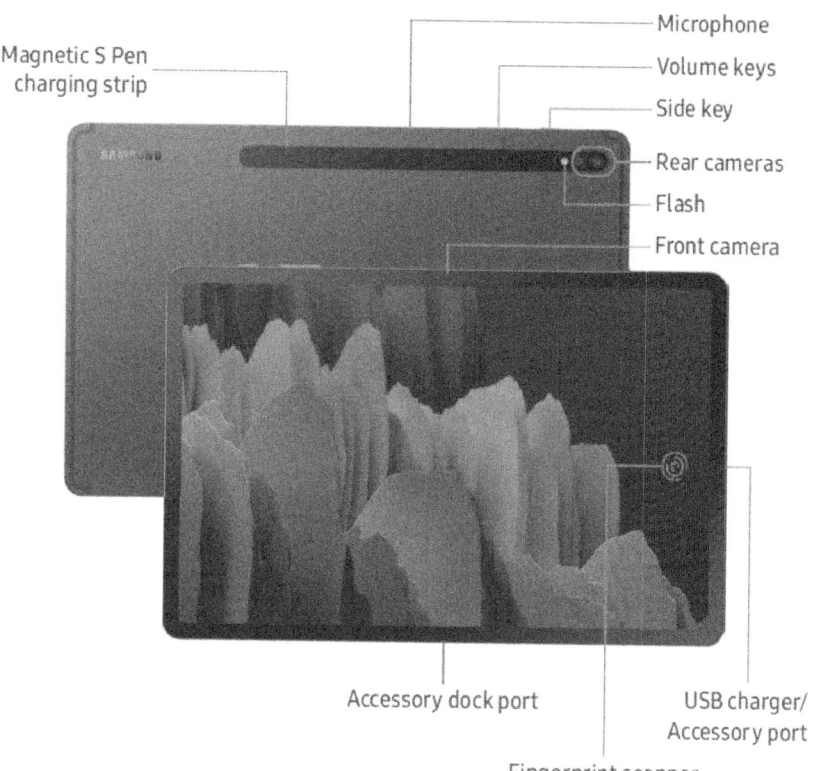

## Unboxing the Galaxy Tab S7 and S7+

The Samsung Galaxy Tab S7 and S7+ come with everything you need to get started with your new Device. Below is a list of things you would see in the box:

1. The Device
2. Travel adapter
3. Data cable
4. SIM Card Eject Tool

The Galaxy Tab S7 and S7+ make use of a Nano-sim. It may also come with a preinstalled sim called eSIM.

**What is an eSIM?**

It is a newly developed technology that allows you to easily switch between carriers and have more than one phone number on your mobile phone. An eSIM, which stands for "embedded subscriber identity module," is a small electronic chip implanted into a mobile device to serve the same function as the little plastic SIM cards.

1: Getting Started 5

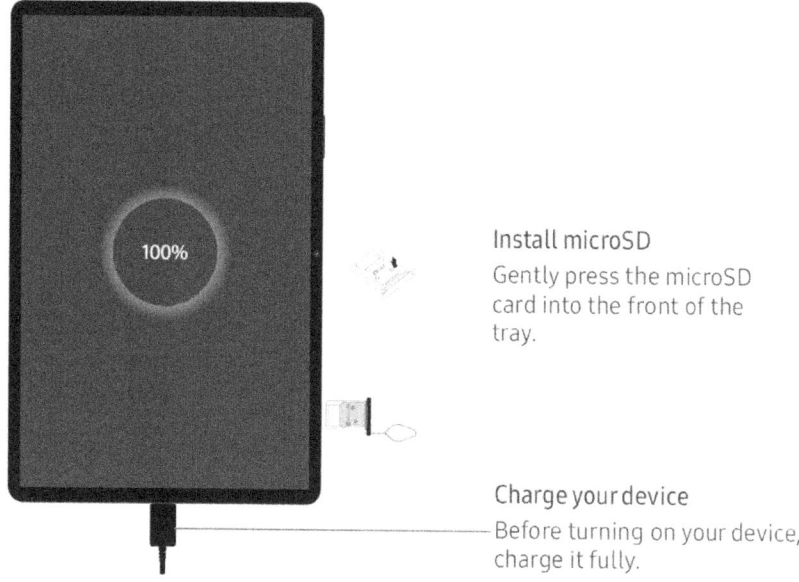

Install microSD
Gently press the microSD card into the front of the tray.

Charge your device
Before turning on your device, charge it fully.

## Power on Your Device

To turn on your device, use the **side key** button. It is recommended that you repair your Device in cases where the body is broken or cracked before powering it on.

Follow the steps below to turn on, power off, and restart your Device.

- Press and hold the **side key** button to turn on your Device.
    - To power off your device, open the device notification panel by swiping down from the top of the device screen, tap the ⏻ Power icon > ⏻ Power off. Confirm your actions when prompted. Note that you can also turn off your

Device by holding, at the same time, the **side** and **volume down** keys.
- To restart your device, open the device notification panel, tap the ⏻ Power icon > ↻ Restart. Confirm your actions when prompted.

## Setting up Your Galaxy Tab S7 and S7+

When you first turn on your device, you may need to set up a few things to get started. The steps below will work you through the setup process of your Galaxy Tab S7 and S7+ devices.

1. Select your language at the 'Let's go!' screen, then tap the **blue arrow** to go to the next stage.
2. Review the terms and conditions, tap on '**I have read and agree to all of the above**,' then tap **next**.
3. Select a Wi-Fi network. You might be prompted to put in your password. When you're done, tap **Next**. You could also choose to skip and add the Wi-Fi networks after setup is complete.
4. Select the preferred option from the 'Copy apps & data' screen. Tap '**Don't copy**' to skip this section.
5. Sign in to your Google account, then hit next to continue. You can also skip this process by tapping

'**skip**.' If you choose 'skip,' then you can add your Google account after you're done with the setup process.

6. From the 'Google Services' screen, you can turn off 'Use location,' 'Allow scanning,' or 'Send usage and diagnostic data' depending on the services you find unnecessary. Tap '**more**' and then '**Accept**' to continue.

7. From the 'Protect your phone' screen, select your preferred option, or you can choose to do it later by tapping '**skip**.' Click '**Next**' on the 'Get recommended apps' screen.

8. From the 'Sign in to your Samsung account' screen, insert your login details to sign in to an existing account, or you can create a new one. If you choose to skip, then you can add a Samsung account when the whole setup process is complete. Tap '**finish**.'

## Transfer Data from Your Old Devices

You can transfer data from an old phone to your new Galaxy Tab S7 and S7+ by making use of the Samsung Smart Switch. The Samsung Smart Switch lets you smoothly transfer all the content in your old phone (such as contacts, messages, pictures, and videos) to your new device. You can use this method to transfer data through USB cable, Wi-Fi, or computer. We'll be looking at how you can transfer data via USB cable and Wi-Fi.

Note that by using Smart Switch, you can only transfer content from your old phones to Samsung Galaxy devices only.

### Transferring Data via USB Cable

This method is best for individuals who do not have a lot of content to transfer from their old phones. If you have years' worth of information, then transferring such data via USB cable wouldn't be the best option since your devices can't be connected to a charger during the process. So for large data, transferring data via Wi-Fi would be the best option.

1: Getting Started  9

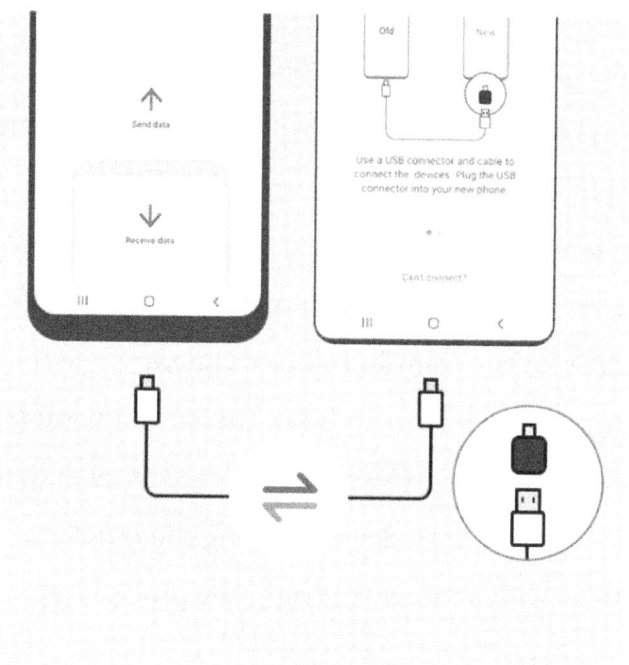

Note: A USB connector (i.e., a USB-OTG adapter) might be required to connect your new galaxy device to your old phone. A USB-OTG adapter can be found in-box with the Galaxy Z flip, Note10+, Note10+ 5G, S10+, S10, and S10e. Follow the steps below to transfer content via a USB cable:

1. By making use of your old phone's USB cable, connect both devices. Most USB cables will require you to make use of an **adapter** to **connect your new Device**.

2. Now, launch the **Smart Switch app** on both devices. You can download and install it if you don't have it already installed.

3. On the old Device, tap **Send data**, and on the new one, tap **Receive data**. Select **Cable** on both devices, and then Smart Switch will X-ray the old phone for transferrable data.
4. Choose the content you'd like to transfer to your new Device. You'd see an approximation of the time it will take for the transfer to be complete. If the transfer time is more than an hour, then it is advisable to go through the wireless transfer process such that you can charge both devices during the transfer.
5. When you're ready to begin the process, tap **Transfer**.
6. At the end of the process, tap **Done** on the new Device and tap **Close** on the old one.

**Transferring Data via Wi-Fi**

When it comes to individuals with a lot of content to transfer, using wireless transfer becomes the best option. This method is fast and makes it possible for your devices to be plugged into a charger during the transfer.

Follow the steps below to transfer content through Wi-Fi:

1. Install the Smart Switch app on both devices and plug both phones into their chargers while ensuring they are within 4 inches of each other.

2. When ready, launch the Smart Switch app on both phones. On the old Device, tap **Send data,** and on the new one, tap **Receive data,** and then select **Wireless** on both devices. On your new phone, you may have to select the type of old Device you're using. Follow the on-screen directions as some types of devices may require extra steps.
3. Complete the connection between both phones by tapping **Allow** on the old Device.
4. On your new Device, select the data you want to move, and when you're ready to begin the process, tap **Transfer.**
5. When the process is complete, tap **Done** on the new phone, and you're all good!

## Lock and Unlock Your Device

You can use your device screen feature to prevent unauthorized access to your Device. By default, the Device locks automatically after being idle for a specified period.

Side key
Press to lock.
Press to turn on the screen, and then swipe the screen to unlock it.

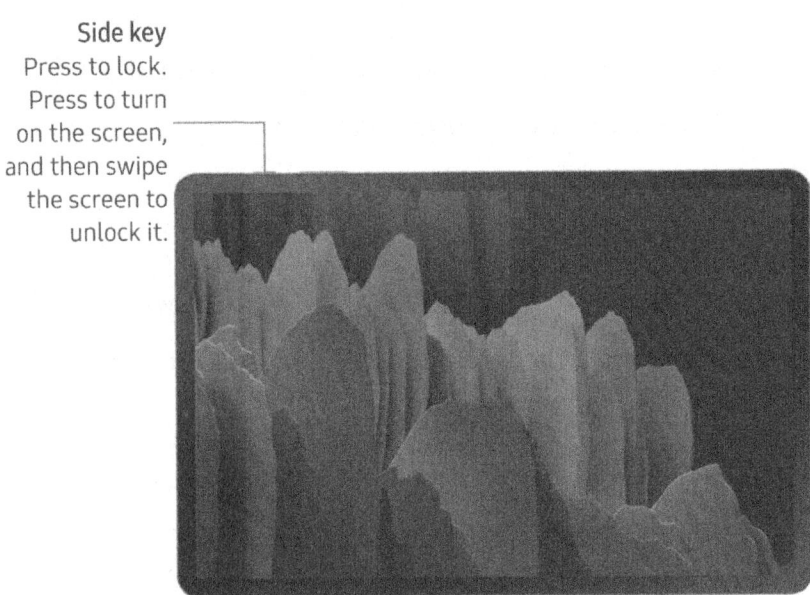

### Types of Screen Lock

There are different screen lock types you can choose to adopt to deny access to the unauthorized use of your phone. We'll be looking at each of them, including the ones that offer no security. These include None, Swipe, Pattern, PIN, and Password.

## Securing Your Device with Screen Lock

It is recommended that you make use of a secure screen lock type like Pattern, PIN, and Password to secure your Device. This also becomes necessary when you want to set up and enable Biometric Security. Follow the steps below to secure your device with a screen lock:

1. From ⚙ **settings**, click 🔒 **Lock screen** > **screen lock type** and choose a secure screen lock type of your choice (e.g., Pattern, PIN, or Password).
   - **Pattern:** A pattern for unlocking your Device is created to allow access to it. To use this screen lock type:
     - Draw a pattern that connects at least four (4) dots, then click **continue.**
     - Draw the exact pattern again and then click **confirm**.
   - **PIN:** A numeric PIN created to access your Device when it is locked. To use it:
     - Input a numeric PIN of 4 to 16 digits, then click **continue.**
     - Enter the same numeric PIN again and click **Done**.

- **Password:** A password that is a combination of numbers and alphabet is created to access your Device when locked. To use it:
    - Input a password of 4 to 16 characters with at least one letter, then click **continue**. Click the 👁 **Show password icon** to view the password as it is being entered.
    - Enter the same password again and click **OK**.

2. Click ⬤ to enable notifications to show up on the lock screen. Depending on how you want the notifications to display on the lock screen, the following options are available:
    - **View style**: Here, you can choose to show notification details or hide them and display only an icon.
    - **Hide content**: Notifications are not displayed in the notification panel.
    - **Notifications to Show**: Select the notifications to display on the lock screen.
    - **Show on 'Always on Display'**: Shows notifications on the 'Always on Display' screen.

3. Click **Done** when finished.
4. Configure other lock screen options to your desire.
    - **Smart Lock:** Unlock your Device automatically when it's in a **trusted location** or detects other **trusted devices** nearby. To use this feature, a secure screen lock type (Pattern, PIN, or Password) is required.
        - To add trusted places, go to settings and click 🔒 **lock screen** > **Smart Lock** > **Trusted places** > **Add trusted places** and choose one or more locations where you want your Device to unlock automatically.
        - To add trusted devices, go to settings and click 🔒 **lock screen** > **Smart Lock** > **Trusted devices** > **Add trusted devices** and choose the devices that would keep your phone unlocked when detected (e.g., Bluetooth watch, headphones, speakers, etc.).
    - **Secure lock settings:** To use this feature, a secure screen lock is required. To modify your secure lock settings to your desire, go to

settings and click 🔒 **lock screen > Secure lock settings** and enter your Pattern, PIN, or Password. You can toggle on **Lock instantly with Side key** so you can easily lock your Device using the side key. You can also choose to toggle on **Lock network and security**, so you can easily track your phone when stolen.

- **Always On Display:** You can view miss calls and message notifications, check time and date, and view other customized data without unlocking your phone using Always on Display (AOD). To enable this feature, go to settings and click 🔒 **lock screen > Always On Display.** Click ⬤ to switch on this feature — it is off by default, and adjust the following options to preference:

  - Choose when to display notifications and a clock on the screen when your device is on standby, i.e., when the screen is off. You can opt for it to **show on schedule** — perhaps only show when you're at work, to show only when you tap on your phone, i.e., **Tap to show,** or to show at all times, i.e., **show always.** Before making a choice, keep in mind that this feature consumes battery.

- **AOD clock style:** There is a range of different clock types and color options you can choose for your Always On Display (AOD) and Lock screen.
- **Show music information:** When the FaceWidgets music controller is in use, you can choose to show music details. The name 'FaceWidgets' is what Samsung uses to represent other information on your lock screen and AOD. The music controller should be there by default, but if it isn't, you can add it by going to **settings** > **Lock screen** > **FaceWidgets**. Here, you'd see the option to turn on or off various features, including weather, Bixby Routines, alarms, and schedules.
- **Rotate Screen:** You can choose to display the AOD in landscape or

portrait mode depending on your preference.

- **Brightness:** You can change the brightness of the AOD from its default type, which is linked to the auto brightness on your phone, to the manual options where you can set it yourself. To do this, go to **settings** > **Lock screen** > **Always On Display**. Here, you'd find "auto brightness." Turn this off and adjust the brightness to preference.

## Biometric Security

Use biometric security to secure your Device and log in to accounts. It may be useful to note that biometrics aren't foolproof because your Device would always revert to Pattern, PIN, or Password to unlock whenever it fails. Thus, your Device is only as secure as the Pattern, PIN, or Password you use since anyone trying to get access to your phone can skip right to these unlock methods. In summary, biometrics are there, not for security, but convenience.

### Face Recognition

You can make use of face recognition to unlock your device. To use your face to gain access to your Device, you must set a secure screen lock (Pattern, PIN, or Password). Before enabling this feature, there are a few things to consider:

- Face Recognition is not as secure as Pattern, PIN, or Password. Someone could gain access to your Device by using something or someone that looks like your image.
- Some conditions can affect the effectiveness of this feature, including heavy make-ups, wearing glasses, beards, or hats.
- To increase this feature's effectiveness, when registering your face, make sure the camera lens is clean, and the environment is bright enough.

To enable this feature:

1. Go to settings and click **biometrics and security > Face Recognition**.
2. Follow the pop-up instructions to register your face.

### Managing Face Recognition

There are a bunch of things you can modify to customize how face recognition works. To do this, go to settings and click ⛨ **biometrics and security** > **Face Recognition**. Here, the followings options are available:

- **Remove face data:** Erase existing face data.
- **Add alternative look:** You can boost face recognition by adding alternative looks so that when next you're wearing sunglasses, your Device won't pull up the 'I don't know you' stunt.
- **Face unlock:** Tap this icon ⬤ to enable or disable face recognition.
- **Stay on Lock screen:** Enable this feature to unlock your Device and stay on the Lock screen (that has been unlocked) until you're ready to swipe.
- **Faster Recognition:** Turn on this feature for faster face recognition. Turn off to increase security and reduce the risk of a video or image being erroneously recognized as your face.
- **Require opened eyes:** This feature improves security and only allows your face to be recognized when your eyes are opened. As a result, unauthorized users cannot gain access to your Device when you're asleep.

- **Brighten screen:** Temporarily increase screen brightness so that your face can be recognized when you're in the dark.
- **Samsung pass:** Gain access to your online accounts by making use of face recognition.
- **About unlocking with biometrics:** Get more information about how you can secure your device using biometrics.

## Using Fingerprint

Aside from face recognition, you can make use of your fingerprints to gain access to your Device and also verify your identity when logging in to your online accounts. To use this feature, you must set a secure screen lock (Pattern, PIN, or Password). To enable this feature:

1. Go to settings and click  **Biometrics and security > Fingerprints.**
2. Follow the pop-up instructions to register your fingerprint.

## Managing Fingerprint

You can add, rename, or delete a fingerprint. To do this, you'd go to settings and click  **Biometrics and security > Fingerprints** to get the following options:

- The first thing you'd see would be the list of registered fingerprints.
- **Add fingerprint:** You can register another fingerprint for extra convenience. It is preferable to register at least one fingerprint from both hands such that you can easily unlock your Device while holding it with either hand.
- **Check added fingerprints:** Check if your fingerprints have been registered by scanning them.
- **Fingerprint unlock:** Tap this icon to enable or disable unlocking your Device with fingerprints.
- **Show icon when screen is off:** Display the fingerprint icon when the Device's screen is off — note that the Always On Display feature has to be enabled for this to work. When you click on **Show icon when screen is off**, select **On Always On Display** to keep the fingerprint sensor visible at all times (only available on the Samsung Galaxy Tab S7+).
- **Show animation when unlocking:** This feature displays an animation whenever you make use of fingerprint verification to unlock your Device (only available on the Samsung Galaxy Tab S7+).

- **Fingerprint always on:** You can wake and, at the same time, unlock your Device by simply touching the side key (only available on the Samsung Galaxy Tab S7).
- **Samsung Pass:** Verify your identity when using supported apps by making use of your fingerprint.
- **About unlocking with biometrics:** Get more information on the requirements each biometric security feature has for making use of your Pattern, PIN, or Password as fallback security.

**Biometrics Preferences**

You can configure your biometric security options according to what you prefer. To do this, go to settings and click **biometrics and security** > **Biometrics preferences** and edit the following option to preference.

- **Screen transition effect**: By enabling this feature, you'd get a beautiful transition effect whenever you unlock your Device using biometrics — i.e., using Face Recognition or Fingerprint to unlock your device.

Note: You can view the software version of your Device's biometric security features by going to Settings > **Biometrics and security** > **Biometrics security patch.**

## Remapping the Side Key Function

You can assign a shortcut to the side key button, such that whenever you press it once, twice, or press and hold, it performs specific functions. The side key in Galaxy Tab S7 and S7+ is a combination of the power key and the Bixby key. The side key of your Device supports four gestures, and we'll be looking at each of them.

1. **Single Press:** This gesture is not customizable. It only functions to wake up or turn off the screen. It can also be configured to instantly lock the screen as explained in **Secure lock settings** under the subheading **Securing Your Device with Screen Lock** (*see* page 15).
2. **Double press:** Choose what feature is launched whenever you double press the side key. To do this:
    - Go to settings, and click ⚙ **Advance features > Side key.**
    - Click on **Double press** to enable (or disable) this feature and tap to choose an option:
        - **Quick launch camera (default):** To open the camera app.
        - **Open Bixby:** To open the Bixby page.

- **Open app:** To open any app of your choice.
3. **Press and hold:** Choose what feature is launched whenever you press and hold the side key (Note that this gesture can't be turned off). To do this:
    - Go to settings, and click ✱ **Advance features** > **Side key.**
    - Under **press and hold,** tap to choose an option:
        - **Wake Bixby:** This option is, by default, the feature that gets launched whenever you press and hold the side key.
        - **Power off menu:** It is recommended that you select this option if you're not a heavy Bixby user so that you can easily turn off your device by pressing and holding the side key.
4. **Press and hold the side and volume keys:** The side key button performs other functions when held simultaneously with the volume down or up keys. Note that this feature isn't customizable, and each combination of the side key and volume keys has a specific function.

- **Press and hold the side and volume-up keys:** When turned off, you can reboot the Galaxy Tab devices into recovery mode by pressing and holding the side and volume up keys simultaneously.
- **Press and hold the side and volume-down keys:**
  - You can simultaneously press and hold the side and volume-down keys for two seconds or less to take a screenshot (*see* page 136).
  - You can power off your Device by simultaneously pressing and holding the side and volume-down keys for longer than seven seconds. This feature also works even when your Device is not responsive.
  - To get to the power off menu, press and hold the side and volume-down keys for a few seconds — greater than two but less than seven seconds.

## Customize the Home Screen

The Home screen is the start off point for navigating your Device. Here, you can place your favorite widgets and apps, add and remove Home screens, change the order of screens, and choose the main Home screen. We'll be looking at App icons, widgets, easy mode, status bar, notification panel, how to create and use folders, customize the home screen by using themes and wallpaper, home screen settings, etc.

### App Icons

You can launch apps from any Home screen by using the app icons. To do this:

- Go to your app list and touch and hold an app icon. Tap  **Add to Home** to add the app icon to the Home screen.

- To remove an icon from the Home screen, touch and hold any icon on the Home screen and tap  **Remove from Home**. Removing an app icon doesn't delete the app itself but only removes the icon from the Home screen.

## How to Create and Use Folders

You can organize app shortcuts (or app icons) in folders on the Home screen. For more material on this subject, see **Create a New Folder** on page 59 of this book.

## Wallpaper

Change the look and feel of your Lock and Home screens by picking your favorite pictures, pre-loaded wallpapers, or videos. To do this:

1. Touch and hold any part of the Home screen, and then click **Wallpaper**.
2. From the list of available options, select one of the following for wallpaper choices.
   - **My wallpapers:** Select from a list of featured and downloaded wallpapers.
   - **Gallery:** Choose from your saved pictures and videos in the Gallery app.
   - **Wallpaper services:** Enable added features, including Dynamic Lock screen and guide page.
   - **Apply Dark mode to Wallpaper:** Enable this feature to apply **Dark mode** to your wallpaper.

- **Explore more wallpapers:** Search for and download new wallpapers from Galaxy themes.
3. When it comes to saved pictures and videos, tap either one to select them.
    - If you're selecting a single picture, choose what screen or screens you want to apply them to as wallpapers.
    - Videos and multiple pictures can only be applied as wallpapers to the Lock screen.
4. Depending on which screen you want to apply the wallpaper to, tap **Set on Home screen**, **Set on Lock screen**, or **Set on Home and Lock screens**.
    - When it comes to applying wallpaper to both the Home and Lock screens, you can enable **Sync my edits** if you want any edit you make to that wallpaper to be functional on both screens.

## Themes

Select a theme that will be applied to your app icons, wallpapers, and Home and Lock screens. To do this:

1. Touch and hold any part of a Home screen, and then tap **Themes** to modify to preference.
2. To preview and download a theme to **My themes**, tap on it.

3. Go to 👤 **My page** > **Themes** to see your downloaded themes.

4. To apply a theme, tap on the theme, and then tap **Apply**.

Icons

You can change the look of icons such that they look different from the default ones. To apply different icon sets to replace the default ones:

1. Touch and hold any part of a Home screen, and then tap 🚩 **Themes** > **Icons** to modify to preference.

2. To preview and download an icon set to **My icons**, tap on it.

3. Go to 👤 **My page** > **Icons** to see your downloaded icons.

4. To apply an icon set, tap on an icon, and then tap **Apply**.

**Widget**

You can add widgets to your Home screen to get easy access to information or apps. Follow the steps below to add widgets to a Home screen:

1. Touch and hold any part of a Home screen.

2. Tap **Widgets**, touch and hold a widget of your choice and drag the selected widget to a Home screen before releasing.

Customize Widgets

After you've successfully added a widget to a Home screen, it's now time to customize its function and location.

- Touch and hold a widget from a Home screen, and select an option:

    - **Remove from Home:** This function deletes a widget from your screen.

    - **Widget settings:** Select this option to customize the appearance and function of the widget.

    - **App info:** Review usage, permission, and more about the selected widget.

**Home screen settings**

You can customize your App and Home screens by going to the Home screen settings. To get there:

1. Touch and hold any part of a Home screen.
2. Click on **Home screen settings** to customize the following to preference:

- **Home screen layout:** Choose whether you want your Device to have separate Apps and Home screens, or if you'd prefer only a Home screen with all your apps located in it.
- **Home screen grid:** Choose a layout to define how you want icons on the Home screen to be arranged.
- **Apps screen grid:** Choose a layout to define how you want icons on the App screen to be arranged.
- **Apps button:** You can add a button to the Home screen to give you easy access to the Apps screen.
- **App icon badges:** Enable this feature to allow badges to show on apps with active notifications. You can also select your preferred badge style.
- **Lock Home screen layout:** Enable this feature to prevent items or icons on the Home screen from being repositioned or removed.
- **Add apps to Home screen:** Enable this feature to automatically add an app icon to the Home screen when newly-downloaded.

- **Swipe down for notification panel:** By enabling this feature, you can swipe down from anywhere on the Home screen to open the notification panel.
- **Rotate to landscape mode:** Automatically rotate the Home screen whenever you change the device orientation from portrait to landscape or vice versa.
- **Hide apps:** You can choose the apps you want to hide from the Home and Apps screens. To restore hidden apps, go back to this screen. Keep in mind that hidden apps are still installed and can return as results in finder searches.
- **About Home screen:** Tap this option to check version information.

**Status Bar**

The Status bar is located at the top end of your screen. It provides you with information on your Device at the right-hand side and notification alerts at the left-hand side of your screen.

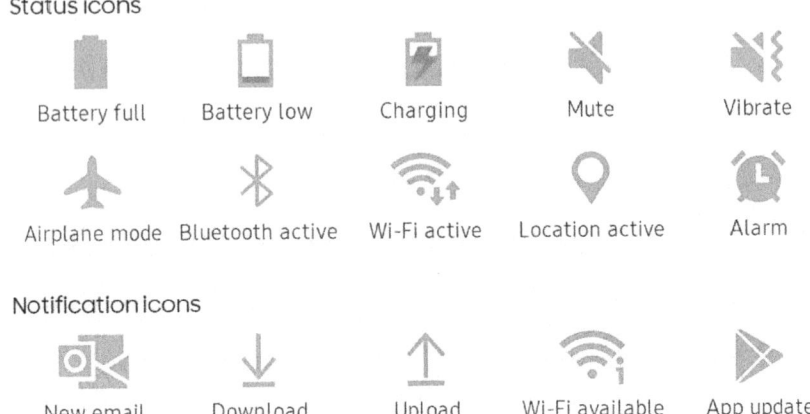

To Configure what would be displayed on the Status bar:

- Go to Quick settings by swiping down from the top of your screen, and tap **More options** > **Status bar** to get the following options:
    - **Show notification icons:** Choose how notification icons would be displayed on the status bar.
    - **Show battery percentage:** Show the battery charge percentage right next to the battery icon on the right-hand side of the status bar.

## Notification Panel

To gain easy access to the power off menu, notifications, settings, and lots more, simply open the notification panel by swiping down from the top of your device screen.

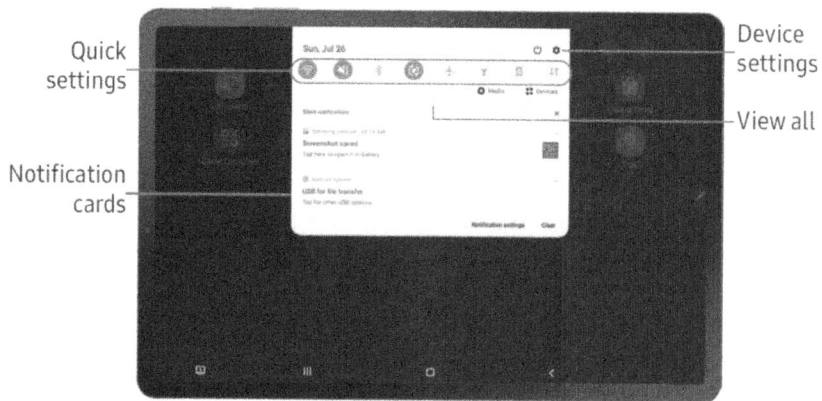

Accessing the Notification Panel

You can view the notification panel from any screen on your Device. To access and navigate the notification panel:

1. Swipe down from the top of the screen (i.e., the status bar region) to display the notification panel.
2. Scroll down through the list to view notification details.
    - Tap on an item to open it.
    - Drag left or right to clear a single notification.
    - Tap **Clear** to clear all notifications.
    - Tap **Notification settings** to customize notifications.

3. To close the notification panel, swipe upward from the bottom of the screen, or tap ⟨ **Back** at the bottom right corner of the screen.

## Quick settings

The Notification panel gives you easy access to your device functions via Quick settings.

1. Swipe down from the top of the screen (i.e., the status bar region) to display the notification panel.
2. Drag down — **View all** (refer to the previous image).
    - To turn on a quick setting icon, tap on it.
    - You can open the main setting of a quick setting icon when you touch and hold it.
    - To search your Device for anything, including settings, apps, calendar appointments, contacts, and so on, tap ⌕ **Finder search** and type in your query.
    - Tap ⏻ **Power off** to turn off, restart, and for other emergency mode options.
    - To gain easy access to the Device's settings menu, tap ⚙ **Open settings**.

- To rearrange Quick settings or to customize the button layout, tap ⋮ **More options.**

3. Drag up — **View all** to close Quick settings.

# 2

# The S Pen -- Samsung's Magic Wand

The S Pen is a jaw-dropping special stylus amalgamated into the Samsung Galaxy Note series. It has been a unique accessory to the Samsung Galaxy Note series since it first premiered in 2011.

The S Pen operates almost like the magic wand from the blockbuster movie, Harry Potter. And yes, it also works on the Samsung Galaxy Tab S7 and S7+. By making some wand-like gesture, it unlocks your Device's power and gives you total control over your Samsung Galaxy Tab.

The Samsung Galaxy S Pen now offers a real pen-like feel, thanks to lower latency and AI-based point prediction. The S Pen also provides diverse useful functions such as: drawing a picture, launching an app, notes, etc.

Note: When your Samsung Galaxy Tab device is close to a magnet, some S Pen functions may not work, such as tapping the touchscreen or charging.

S Pen button

## Air Actions

You can perform remote functions with your S Pen by using the button, movements, and gestures. You can use it to navigate your Device's screen, set up shortcuts to your favorite apps, complete actions, and so much more!

Your S Pen remote feature uses Bluetooth Low Energy. So, if your S Pen is too far from your Device or there is some sort of interference, the S Pen will disconnect from your Samsung Galaxy device. For Air action to work, the S Pen must be connected to your Samsung Galaxy device.

**Press and hold shortcut**

Set up a shortcut when you press and hold the S Pen button.

- Go to Settings, then tap ✲ **Advanced features** > **S Pen** > **Air actions**.
- Tap **Hold down Pen button to** and toggle ⬤ the switch to enable this feature.
- Then tap an option to set the shortcut.

**Anywhere actions**

Anywhere actions are new Air actions that are available on your Samsung Galaxy note device. It enables you to navigate your smartphone without touching it. They are configurable shortcuts that you can access simply by making one of these gestures: left, right, up, down, or shake.

You can access these from any screen and can include navigation, apps, or S Pen features.

| | Action | Gesture |
|---|---|---|
| ‹ | Back | Left to right |
| ||| | Recent Apps | Right to left |
| ◯ | Home | Up and down |

 **Smart Select**   Down and up

 **Screen Write**   Zigzag

You can configure or customize the Anywhere actions in Settings

- Go to Settings, then tap ⚙ **Advanced features** > **S Pen** > **Air actions.**
- Then under Anywhere actions, you can tap a gesture icon to customize the shortcut.

**App actions**

This enables you to do specific actions in certain apps with your S Pen. The table below shows some of the default App options.

|  | Single press | Double press | Up/Down | Left/Right | Rotate |
|---|---|---|---|---|---|
| **Camera** | Take picture | Switch cameras | Switch cameras | Next/Previous mode | Zoom in/Out |
| **Gallery** | Next | Previous | View details | Next/Previous |  |
| **Media** | Play/Pause | Play next | Volume up/down | Play previous/Next |  |

You can change and customize the App actions in Settings.

- Go to Settings, then tap ✱ **Advanced features** > **S Pen** > **Air actions.**
- Tap an App to see the available shortcuts.
- Toggle ⬤ the switch to enable the shortcut while using the app.

**General app actions**

Under here, you can change and customize some general actions while using Camera and media apps not specified in the app action list.

- Go to Settings, then tap ✱ **Advanced features** > **S Pen** > **Air actions.**
- Then under General app actions, tap an action to change it.

# Air View

Access this feature by hovering the S Pen nib over the screen and quickly and conveniently preview contents or information about an item on your screen. Air view saves you time and energy, making it easier to manage your life's contents.

Hover the Pen over your screen to avail the following Air view features:

- Use it to preview a video and navigate to a specific scene by hovering over the video's timeline.
- Use it to preview an email message before opening it.
- Use it to preview the contents of a photo album or as zoom control by hovering over an image for a while.
- Use it to view the description and name of an icon by hovering the Pen near the icon.

Note: When the S Pen's on-screen pointer is a solid color, it indicates that the preview function is available.

## Air Command

Air command is a menu that provides S Pen signature features and quick access to frequently used apps like Samsung note, PENUP, Smart select, etc. You can access the Air command panel or menu from any screen by simply holding the S Pen close to your screen so that the pointer appears, and then press the S Pen button once.

Alternatively, you can also tap the air command floating icon that pops up when you activate the S Pen.

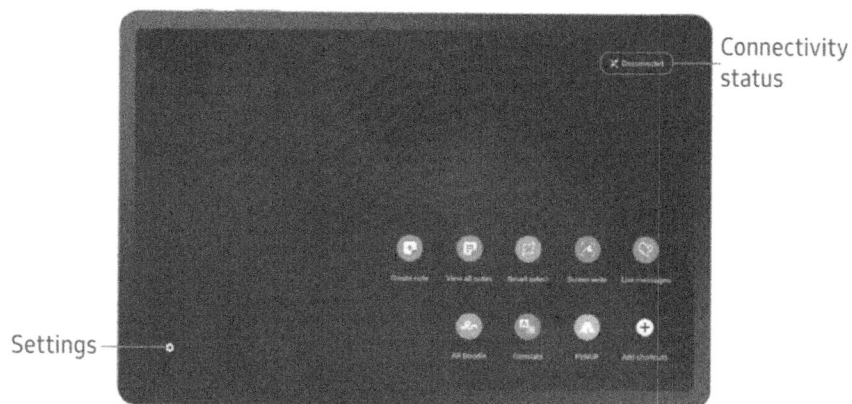

The following are the S Pen features and apps that you can access through Air command:

- **Create note**: Start a new note in the Samsung Notes app.

- **View all notes**: Open the Samsung Note app and view a listing of the note you have previously created.

- **Smart select**: Draw around a content to copy it and add it to your Gallery app.

- **Screen write**: Write or draw on captured screenshots.

- **Live messages**: Draw or write with the S Pen to create a short animated message.

- **AR Doodle**: Use the AR camera feature to draw interactive doodles.

- **Translate**: Translate a word and listen to its pronunciation by hovering the S Pen over the word.

- **PENUP**: Draw, color, edit, and share live drawing with your S Pen.
- **Add shortcuts**: Add more functions or apps to the Air command panel or Menu.
- **Settings**: Customize and configure the apps and function, and change how the Air command panel or menu appears.

**Create notes**

Directly launch a new note in the Samsung Notes app.

- Tap **Air command** > **Create notes**.

**View all notes**

Open the Samsung Note app and view a listing of the note you have previously created.

- Tap **Air command** > **View all notes**.

**Smart select**

Use the Smart select feature to copy content from any screen, which you can then add to your Gallery app or share with your contacts.

1. Tap **Air command** > **Smart select**.

2. Tap and drag the S Pen on the content you want to select, and these options will appear:
    - **Extract text**: Identify and extract text from the selected content for sharing or copying.
    - **Auto select:** This allows Smart select to choose the content to extract automatically.
    - **Draw**: Draw on the selected content.
    - **Share**: Choose your preferred sharing method to share your content.
3. Tap **Save**.

**Screen write**

This feature allows you to write and draw on your screenshots.

1. Tap **Air command** > **Screen write**.
2. Your current screen is captured, and a pen tool appears. These are the editing tools provided:
    - **Crop**: Drag the edges of your screen to crop the screenshot and remove unwanted outer areas.
    - **Pen type**: Tap the Pen icon a second time to change the pen tip, size, and color when drawing.

- **Eraser**: Erase writing or drawing errors on the screenshot. For additional options, including erase all, tap the Eraser icon a second time.
- **Undo**: Reverse the previous action.
- **Redo**: Repeat the previous action that was undone.
- **Share**: Choose your preferred sharing method to share your content.

3. Tap **Save** to save the screenshot to your Gallery app.

Tips & Tricks: Press and hold the **S Pen** button to erase your drawings on the screen memo.

### Live messages

With this feature, you can create an animated drawing or written message.

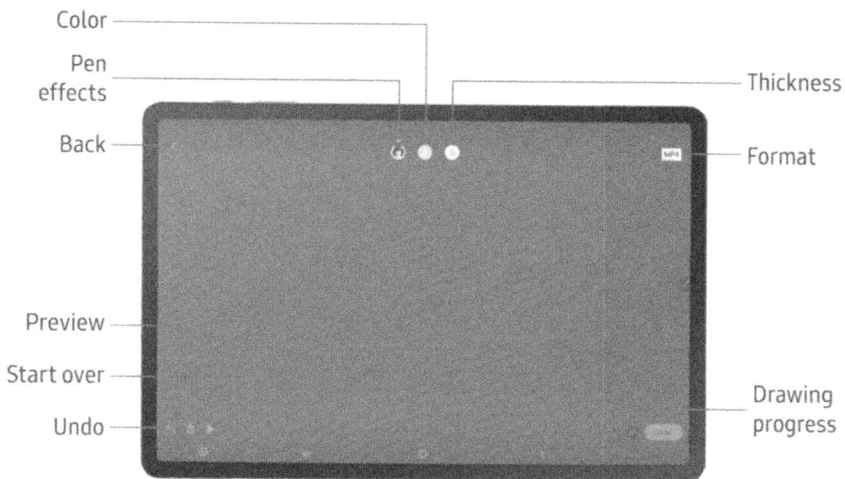

1. Tap  **Air command** >  **Live messages**.
2. Choose one of the following background options:
    - **Collection**: View all Live messages you previously created.
    - **Gallery**: Select an image or video for the background.
    - **Camera**: Snap a picture to use for the background.
    - **Color**: Select a color for the background.
3. Tap **Done** to save your live message.

## AR Doodle

Use Augmented reality to draw interactive doodles on faces or objects seen through the camera.

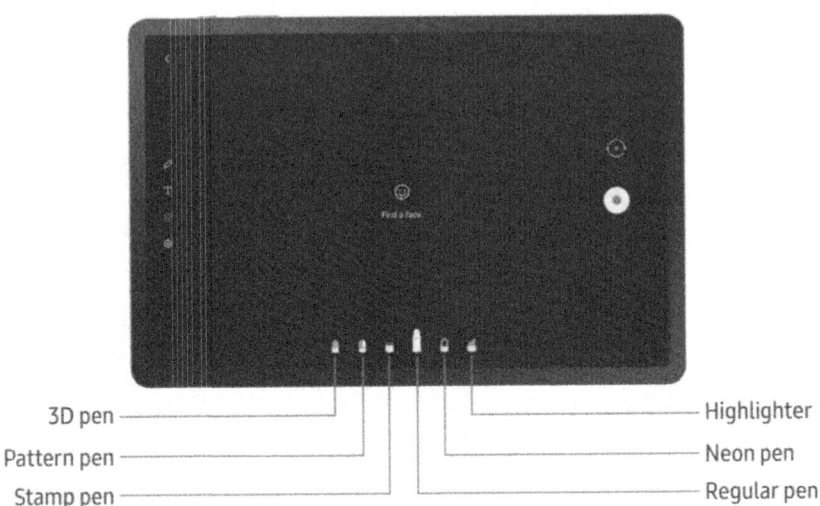

- 3D pen
- Pattern pen
- Stamp pen
- Highlighter
- Neon pen
- Regular pen

1. Tap ✏ **Air command** > **AR Doodle**.
2. Tap ⟳ **Switch camera** to either select the front or rear cameras.
3. Position the camera on your target and make sure it is at the center of your screen.
4. Draw a doodle with your S Pen.
    - The Doodle simultaneously follows the movement of the face.
5. To save a video of your AR Doodle, tap ⏺ **Record**.

**Translate**

With the S Pen, hover over words to translate them and listen to their pronunciation.

1. Tap ✏ **Air command** > **Translate**.

2. Select your preferred source language and your target language.
3. Hover your S Pen over a word to translate it.
    - Tap **Sound** to hear the word pronunciation.
    - Tap **Copy** to save the selected text and its translation to your clipboard.
    - To close translate, tap **Close**.

**PENUP**

This feature allows you to Draw, color, edit, and share live drawings with your S Pen.

1. Tap **Air command** > **PENUP**.

**Add shortcuts**

This feature allows you to customize the Air command menu by adding shortcuts to S Pen features, apps, and functions.

1. Tap **Air command** > **Add shortcuts**.
2. Tap and select the apps and functions you would like to add to the Air command menu.
    - Tap **Remove** to remove an app and function shortcut.
3. Then tap **Back** to save your selection.

## Screen off Memo

Compose notes or ideas wherever and whenever you need to. Screen off memo allows you to write memos without unlocking your Galaxy note device.

1. Pull out the S Pen while the screen is off, and write on the screen.
2. Use these options to customize your memo:
    - **Color**: Change your pen color.
    - **Pen settings**: Tap once to use the pen tool and double-tap to adjust the line thickness.
    - **Eraser**: Tap once to use the eraser too and double-tap to erase all.
3. When done, tap **Save** to save your memo to the Samsung Notes app.

Note: The Screen off memo must be enabled for it to work. To enable, go to S Pen settings and enable Screen off memo.

## Pin to Always on Display

This feature allows you to pin or edit a memo on the Always on Display.

1. From Screen off memo tap **Pin**.
2. Click **Pin to Always on Display**.

## Configure S Pen Settings

To configure and customize your S Pen settings:

- Go to Settings, then tap ✻ **Advanced features** > **S Pen** to configure the following settings:
    - **Air action**: Configure and customize how the remote control functions while using the app.
    - **S Pen unlock**: This allows you to use the S Pen button to unlock your Galaxy note device. You must set a secure screen lock to use this feature.
    - **Screen off memo**: This feature allows you to detach your S Pen, write, and create memos while your screen is off. Screen off memos are saved in Samsung Notes.
    - **Create note with Pen button**: Start a new note by pressing and holding the S Pen button, then tap your screen twice.
    - **Air view**: Turn on or off
    - **Show pointer when hovering**: Turn on or off. The pointer appears on your screen when you bring the S Pen tip close to your screen, showing available options.
    - **Allow other S Pens**: Enable to let other S Pens write on the screen.

### Air command

- **Shortcuts**: Customize the Air command menu by adding shortcuts to S Pen features, apps, and functions.
- **Show floating icon**: Show an Air command floating icon that you can move around the screen.
- **Open Air command with the S Pen**: Open the Air command menu by holding the S Pen close to your screen so that the pointer appears, and then press the S Pen button.

### Removal

- **When S Pen is removed**: Choose what happens when you detach your S Pen. Choose either **Open Air command**, **Create note,** or **Do nothing**.
- **Pen proximity alert**: Set your Device to give a warning alert if you leave your S Pen detached and walk away while the screen is off.

### Feedback

- **Sound**: Enable if you want your Device to make sounds when writing on the screen.

- **Vibration**: Activate vibration feedback whenever you detach and attach the S Pen.

General

- **Tips for using your S Pen**: Find out cool tips and tricks.
- **About S Pen features**: View the version information for the S Pen features.
- **Contact us**: Contact Samsung support via Samsung members.

## Replace the S Pen tip or nib

You can always replace the tip of your S pen (sold separately) whenever it becomes worn out or faulty.

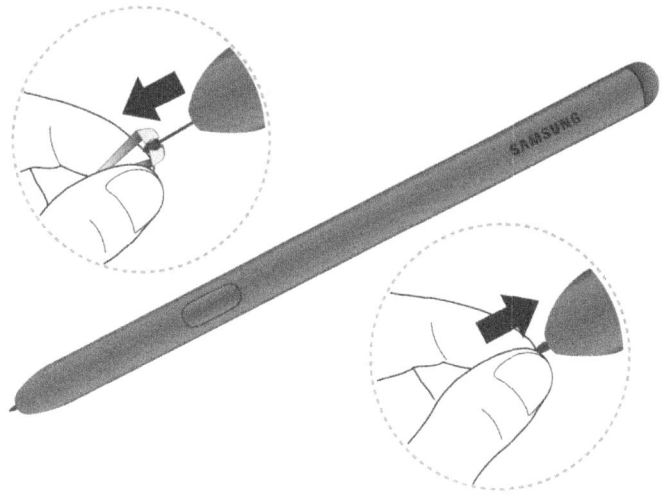

- To remove the tip, hold the tip firmly with the tweezer, then gently pull the tip out.

- Carefully insert a new tip with your fingers. It will insert easily with very little pressure.

Note: You will not hear or feel a click when you install the tip.

# 3

# Using Apps

An app is a software that allows you to perform specific tasks on your mobile device.

## Download Apps

All downloaded and preloaded apps are displayed in the apps list. You can download your desired apps from the Galaxy store and Google play store.

- From your home screen, swipe upwards to access your apps list.

## Disable or Uninstall Apps

Downloaded apps can be uninstalled and removed from your Device. Some preloaded apps (available on your Device by default) cannot be uninstalled; it can only be disabled. Disabled apps are hidden and turned off from your apps list.

- From apps, touch and hold the app you intend to Uninstall or Disable, then tap **Uninstall** or **Disable**.

## Search for Apps

If you're finding it difficult to find an app or a setting, you can conveniently use the search feature to locate that app or setting.

- From apps, tap **search**, input letters or words to spell the app or setting you wish to find.
- The app (if it has been installed on your Device) and setting will be found.
- Tap on the result to go to that app or setting.

NB: You can customize the search settings: Tap on **more options**, then tap **finder settings**.

## Sort Apps

Finding an installed app from a pool of apps can be frustrating. Sorting your apps helps you find an app a lot quicker and easier. Your apps shortcuts can be arranged in alphabetical order or your preferred custom order.

- From apps, tap the more options icon, tap sort for the following sorting options:

- **Alphabetical order:** Sort your apps alphabetically.
- **Custom order:** Arrange your apps manually.

## Create a New Folder

Create new folders to organize your app shortcuts on your apps list.

1. From apps, touch and hold an app shortcut (e.g., Gmail), drag the shortcut on to a different app shortcut (e.g., email)
2. When highlighted, release the shortcut to create a folder.
   - **Folder name:** Name your folder
   - **Palette:** Change your folder color
   - **Add apps:** Add more apps to the folder. Tap the apps you want to add then, tap done.
3. Tap the **back** icon when you are done.

### Moving folder to my home screen

You can move or copy a folder to your home screen with this few steps:

- From apps, long-press the folder you want to copy, then tap **add to Home**.

### Deleting a folder

Know that the apps shortcuts return to the home screen when you delete a folder.

- From apps, long-press the folder you wish to delete
- Tap **delete folder**, then confirm the prompt

## Game Booster

If you're a gamer, this feature was designed just for you.

You can have a better gaming experience with this feature, which optimizes your tablet performance when playing games and provides various tools to improve your gameplay in many ways.

- While playing a game, swipe up from the bottom of your screen (if in portrait mode) or swipe left (if in landscape mode).

- Then tap **Start** to activate.

Using the pop-up panel

The pop-up panel gives you quick access to four apps. This enables you to quickly check a message or watch a YouTube video on how to stop being a big noob.

The pop-up panel is customizable. You can add any installed app to your Device.

- While playing a game, swipe up from the bottom of your screen (if in portrait mode) or swipe left (if in landscape mode)
- Tap the **Game Booster** icon.
- The **pop-up panel** will appear at the top of your screen.
- Tap the more options icon to customize the apps
- To remove an app, tap the remove icon, then tap on the apps you wish to add to the pop-up panel.

Use the Game Booster to block calls and other notifications and enable cool features like Bixby or Dolby Atmos.

## App settings

Use this feature to manage both your downloaded and preloaded apps. Different apps have different configurations or options.

1. From settings, tap on **apps**.
2. Tap the **more options icon** to access the following options:
    - **Sort by:** Sort your apps by either size, name, last used, or last updated.
    - **Default apps:** Select or change the apps that are used as the default for certain tasks like browsing the Internet, Email, etc.
    - **Permission manager**: Control or give permissions to some apps to use certain features of your mobile device.
    - **Show/Hide system apps:** Use this to Show/Hide system background apps.

- **Special access:** Choose which app you want to give special access permission to features on your Device
- **Reset app preferences:** Reset options that have been changed to their default. This won't delete existing app data.

3. Tap an app to view and change information about the app. These options should appear:

**Usage-**
- **Mobile data**: View mobile data used by the app
- **Battery:** View the battery usage by the app since the last full charge.
- **Storage:** View and manage the app's storage usage.
- **Memory:** View the app's memory usage.

**App settings-**
- **Notification:** Configure the app's notification.
- **Permission:** View the permissions that were granted to the app for access to your Device's features.
- **Set as default:** Set the app as default for a certain task.

**Advanced-**

- Different options for every app.

**App info option-**
- **Open:** Launch the app. This option is not available in every app.
- **Uninstall/Disable:** Uninstall or Disable the app. As stated earlier, some preloaded apps cannot be uninstalled and can only be disabled.
- **Force stop:** Force stop the app if it's not working properly.

# 4

# Samsung Apps

The listed apps below make up the Samsung apps. The apps are either preloaded or downloaded over-the-air (OTA) to your mobile Device during set up.

Galaxy Essentials | Bixby | AR Zone | Galaxy store | Game Launcher | PENUP | Samsung Members | SmartThings | Tips | Calculator | Calendar | Clock | Contacts | Internet | Messages | My Files | Phone | Samsung Notes |

## Galaxy Essentials

Galaxy Essentials is a group of specially selected applications that are available through Samsung Apps.

- From your apps, tap the **more options** icon, then tap **Galaxy Essentials**.

## Bixby

Bixby is a virtual assistant. It displays customized content based on your activities. Bixby suggests things you may like by learning and adapting to your usage pattern.

*See* **page 107** for more information on Bixby.

- From your apps, tap **Samsung Folder**, then **tap Bixby**.

## AR Zone

You can access all your Augmented Reality (AR) features here. *See* **page 120** to get more information on AR Zone.

- From your apps, tap **Samsung Folder**, then tap **AR Zone**.

## Galaxy Store

This is an app store that is unique to Galaxy and Gear devices. Search and download premium apps that are exclusive to your Galaxy device.

- From your apps, tap **Galaxy Store**.

NB: You need a Samsung account to download from this app store (Galaxy Store).

## Game Launcher

This app is exclusive to Samsung devices. It arranges the mobile games on your Device conveniently in one place. With this app, you can adjust the game settings to increase user experience or save power and mute and hide alerts.

- From your apps, tap **Game Launcher**.

NB: If you do not see Game launcher in apps, then from settings, tap **Advanced features**, **Game Launcher**, toggle the switch to enable.

## PENUP

This is a social network, a community that brings together people who enjoy drawing, sketching, painting, or scribbling with the S pen. You can share your arts and photos, comment on other creations, or just browse through the pages to find a masterpiece to add to your collection.

- From your app, tap **Samsung** folder > PENUP.

## Samsung Members

This is a support app that contains a community of Galaxy professionals that provide DIY (Do It Yourself) product support, insider tips and tricks, and exclusive experiences and contents for Samsung Members only.

The Samsung Members app may be preloaded on your Device or downloaded and installed from your Google Play Store or Galaxy Store.

- From your apps, tap **Samsung** Folder, then tap **Samsung Members**.

## SmartThings

SmartThings app allows you to connect, automate, and manage all your Samsung and SmartThings-compatible home appliances and electronics. The app is simple and efficient, no matter how many devices it's connected to, thus, providing your specific needs. Check the status of the connected devices by looking at the dashboard.

- From your apps, tap Samsung **Folder,** then tap **SmartThings** and sign in with your Samsung account.

NB: Samsung warranty does not cover non-Samsung connected device defects or errors; for support, contact the non-Samsung device manufacturer.

## Tips

View your Device's tips and techniques.

- From your apps, tap **Tips.**

## Calculator

The Calculator app features both the basic and scientific calculators and also a unit converter.

- From your apps, tap **Calculator**.

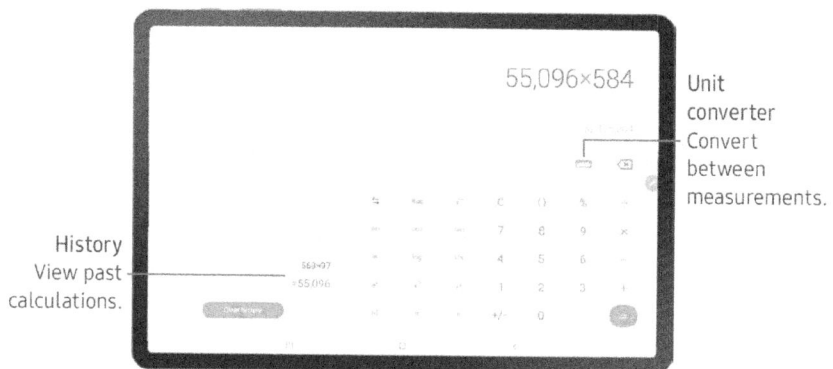

## Calendar

Your Samsung Galaxy's digital Calendar can be connected to your various online account to consolidate all your calendars in just one place, thus, keeping you always on top of your routine.

- From your apps, tap **Calendar**.

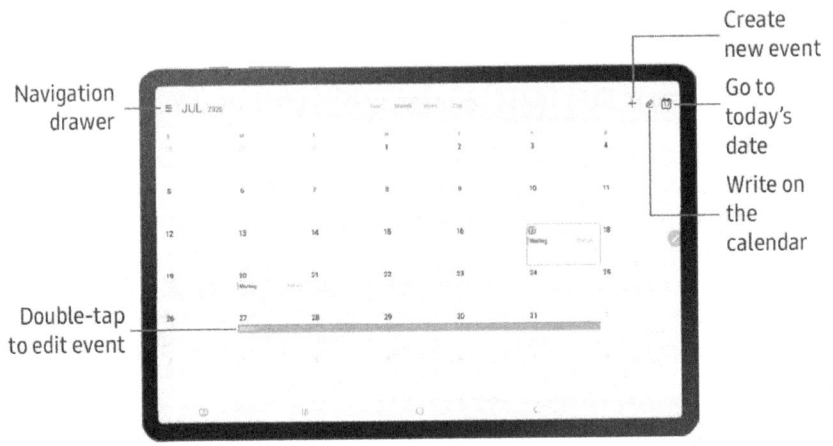

## Add Calendars

Add or connect your online account to the Calendar app.

1. From your **Calendar**, tap the **Navigation drawer** icon at the top left.

2. Tap **Settings**, **Add new account** and choose the account type.

3. Enter your account details and follow the prompts.

## Subscription Calendars

Subscribe to Calendars that meet your interests to easily find upcoming events and include them in your schedule.

1. From **Calendar**, tap the **Navigation drawer** icon at the top left.

2. Then tap **Subscribe to your interest** and follow the prompts.

## Calendar Alert Styles

You can set the Calendar alert to your preferred style.

1. From your Calendar, tap the **Navigation drawer icon** at the top left, tap **Settings** > **Alert styles**. The following options are available:
    - **Light:** Receive a notification and hear a brief sound.
    - **Medium:** Receive a full-screen alert and hear a brief sound.
    - **Strong:** Receive a full-screen alert and a sound that persists until it is dismissed.
2. The sound options available here are dependent on the Alert styles selected above, and they are:
    - **Ring once sound:** This option is available for Light and Medium alert styles.
    - **Keep ringing sound:** This option is available for a Strong alert style.

## Create an Event

1. From your Calendar, tap **Create new event**.
2. Enter the event's details, then tap **Save**.

## Delete an Event

1. From your **Calendar**, tap an event and tap the second time to edit.

2. Tap **Delete** and confirm the prompt.

## Clock

Keep track of time and set alarms with the Clock app.

- From your apps, tap **Clock**.

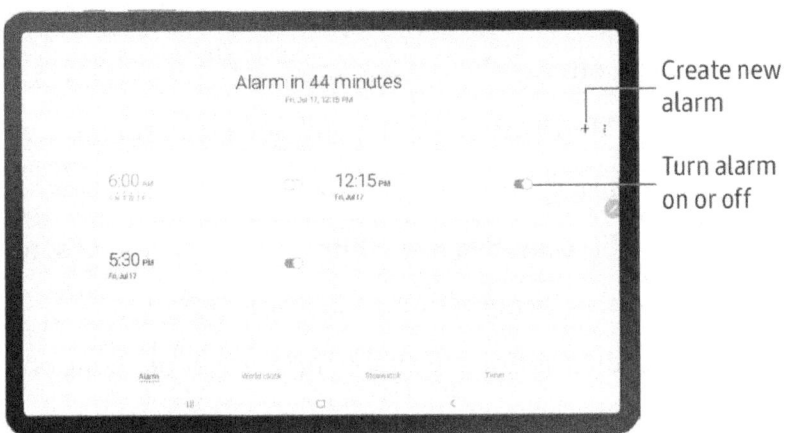

**Alarm**

Use the alarm tabs to set alarms. Set either one time or recurring alarms and choose your preferred options for how to be notified.

1. From the **Clock** app, tap the **Add alarm** icon.
2. Configure or set your alarm with the following items:
    - **Time:** Set a time for your alarm
    - **Day:** Choose the days for your alarm.
    - **Alarm name:** Enter a name for your alarm

- **Alarm sound:** Choose the alarm sound to play and drag the slider to adjust the alarm sound volume.
- **Vibration:** Choose either vibration alert or no vibration alert for your alarm.
- **Snooze:** Delay the alarm for several more minutes with this item.
- To save the alarm, tap **Save**.

**Delete an Alarm**

Delete an alarm you previously created:

1. From the **Clock** app, long-press an alarm
2. Tap **Delete**.

**World clock**

Keep track of the current time in multiple cities around the globe with the World clock.

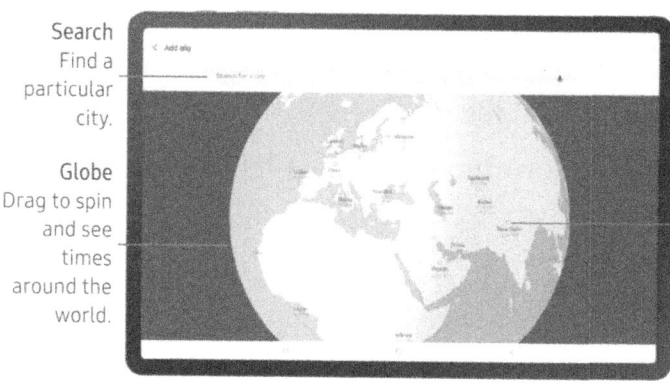

Search — Find a particular city.

Globe — Drag to spin and see times around the world.

City — View the current time and add to your list of cities.

1. From the **Clock** app, tap **World Clock** at the base of your screen.
2. Tap **Add city**, tap **Search for a city**, then enter the city name.
3. Tap the city name and then tap **Add**.
   - To delete a city, long-press the city, then tap **Delete**.

Time Zone Converter

This enables you to set a time on your World clock and to convert the time to the local time of the other cities.

1. From the **Clock** app, tap **World clock** at the base of your screen.
2. Tap the **More options** icon, then **Time zone converter**.
3. Tap **Menu** to select a different city.
   - Tap **add city** to add a city to the list.
4. Swipe your screen to set the hours, minutes, periods (AM or PM) on the Clock.
   - Tap **Reset** to return the Clock to the current time.

## Weather Settings

Show the weather forecast of various cities on your World clock.

1. From the **Clock** app, tap **World clock** at the base of your screen.
2. Tap the **More options** icon, **Settings**, tap **Show weather** to either enable or disable the weather forecast or information.
3. Tap **Temperature** to switch from Fahrenheit to Celsius.

## Stopwatch

A stopwatch lets you time an event, from its time of activation to its time of deactivation.

1. From the **Clock** app, tap **Stopwatch**.
2. To begin timing, tap **Start**
   - Tap **lap** to keep track of lap times.
3. To end timing, tap **Stop.**
   - Tap **Resume** to continue time after stopping the Clock.
   - Tap **Reset** to reset the Stopwatch to zero.

## Timer

Timer lets you set a countdown timer for up to 99 hours, 59 minutes, 59 seconds.

1. From the **Clock** app, tap **Timer**.
2. Set the Timer by using the keypad to tap Hours, Minutes, and Seconds.
3. To begin the Timer, tap **Start**.
    - Tap **Pause** to stop the Timer temporarily. Tap **Resume** to continue.
    - Tap **Cancel** to stop and reset the Timer.

**Preset Timer**

1. From the Clock app, tap **Timer**, then tap **Add preset Timer**.
2. Configure both the countdown time and the timer name.
3. To save the Timer, tap Add.
    - To edit a saved preset timer, tap the **More options** icon (three vertical dots), then tap **Edit preset timer.**

**Timer Options**

Customize your Timer with your preferred choice.

1. From the Clock app, tap **Timer**.
2. Tap the **More options** icon (three vertical dots), then tap **Settings**.

4: Samsung Apps    77

- o **Sound:** Choose or add a preloaded timer sound.
- o **Vibration:** Enable or disable vibration for the Timer

**General settings**

View and configure the settings for all your clock tools.

- From the **Clock** app, tap the **More options** icon (three vertical dots), then tap **Settings.**

# Contacts

This allows you to store and manage your contacts. You can synchronize your account with a personal account (e.g., WhatsApp) added to the Device.

- From your apps, tap **Contacts**, then tap **Create contact.**

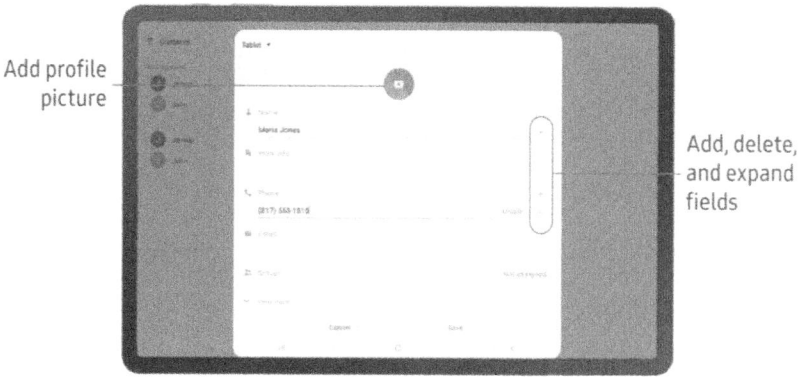

Add profile picture

Add, delete, and expand fields

### Edit a Contact

You edit a contact by tapping a field, then changing and deleting its information, or by adding more information to the field.

1. From **Contacts**, tap the contact you wish to edit.
2. Tap **Edit** (pencil icon).
3. Tap any of the fields to change, delete, or add information.
4. Then tap **Save**.

### Call or Message a Contact

Quickly call or message a contact by using their already saved phone number.

1. From **Contacts**, tap the contact you wish to call or message.
2. Then tap **Call** or **Message**.

### Favorites

Select or mark contacts as your favorites so that they will easily be accessible from other apps.

1. From **Contacts**, tap the contact you wish to add as one of your favorites.
2. Tap **Add as favorite** icon to mark the contact as a favorite.

- Unmark and remove from favorites by tapping **favorite.**

## Share a Contact

Share contacts with friends and family by using various sharing methods.

1. From **Contacts**, tap the contact you wish to share.
2. Tap the **Share** icon.
3. Choose either file or text.
4. Select a sharing method and follow the prompts.

## Direct Share

You can share content directly with a contact within any app. Your frequent contacts will be displayed in the share window once it is enabled.

- From **Settings,** tap **Advanced features,** then **Direct share,** and toggle the switch to enable the feature.

## Groups

Use this feature to organize your contacts in groups.

### Create a group

1. From **Contacts**, tap **Open drawer** (three horizontal lines), then **Groups.**
2. Tap **Create group**, then tap any of the fields to input information about the group.

- o **Group name**: Enter a name for your new group
- o **Group ringtone:** Select the sounds for your new group.
- o **Add member:** Add new members to your group.

3. Tap Save.

Add or remove group contact

- From Contacts, tap Open drawer (three horizontal lines), tap Groups, and then tap a group.
    - o To remove a contact, long-press the contact to select it, then tap **Remove.**
    - o While to add a contact, tap **Edit**, tap **Add number**, then tap the contact you wish to add. Tap **Done** when finished.

Send a message to a group

1. From **Contacts**, tap **Open drawer** (i.e., the "three horizontal lines"), tap **Groups**, and then tap a group.
2. Tap **More options** (i.e., the "three vertical dots"), then tap **Send message**.

Send an email to a group

1. From **Contacts**, tap **Open drawer** (i.e., the "three horizontal lines"), tap **Groups**, and then tap a group.
2. Tap **More options** (i.e., the "three vertical dots"), and tap **send email.**
3. Tap the checkbox to select all contacts in the group or tap each contact to select them.
4. Select an email account and follow the prompts.

NB: Only members in the group with an email address in their records will be displayed.

Delete a group

To delete a group you created, follow these steps:

1. From **Contacts**, tap **Open drawer** (three horizontal lines), tap **Groups**, and then tap a group.
2. Tap **More options** (three vertical dots), then tap **Delete.**
   - Tap **Group only** to delete only the group or tap **Group and members** to delete the group and contacts.

## Manage Contacts

Link multiple contacts into one contact entry and also import and export contact.

Link contacts

Merge contact information from multiple sources into one contact by linking entries into a single contact.

1. From **Contacts**, tap the contact you wish to select.
2. Tap **More options** (three vertical dots), tap **Link to other contacts.**
3. Tap a contact to select them, then tap **Link.**

Unlink contacts

1. From **Contacts**, tap the contact you wish to unlink.
2. Tap **More options** (three vertical dots), and tap **Add/remove linked contact.**
3. Then tap **Unlink** beside contacts to Unlink them from the main contact.

Import contacts

Import contacts to your Samsung Galaxy as vCard files (VCF).

1. From **Contacts**, tap **Open drawer** (three horizontal lines), tap **Manage account.**
2. Tap **Import contacts** and follow the prompts.

Export contacts

Export contacts to your Samsung Galaxy as vCard files (VCF).

1. From **Contacts**, tap **Open drawer** (three horizontal lines), tap **Manage account**.
2. Tap **Export contacts** and follow the prompts.

Delete contacts

Use this to delete single or multiple contacts.

1. From Contacts, long-press any contact to select it.
    - You can also tap and check other contacts to select them for deletion.
2. Tap **Delete** and confirm the prompts.

# Internet

Samsung Internet is a reliable, fast, and user-friendly web browser in your Samsung Galaxy device.

- From your apps, tap **Internet**.

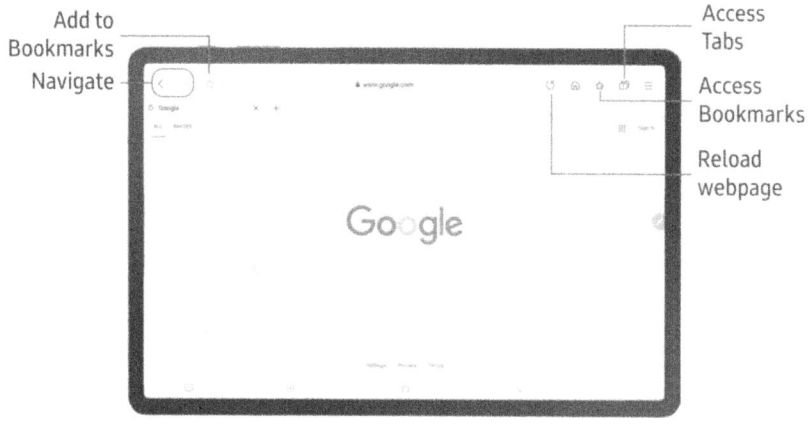

### Browser Tabs

This enables you to view multiple web pages at the same time.

1. From **Internet**, tap **tabs**, then **new tab**.
2. To delete or close a tab, tap **tabs**, then **✗ close tab**.

### Bookmarks

This enables you to store Bookmarks, Save pages, and your browsing history.

### Open a Bookmark

Launch a web page in a jiff from your Bookmark page.

1. From **Internet**, tap **Bookmarks**.
2. Then tap a **bookmark entry**.

### Save a Web Page

Saving a web page stores its content on your mobile device, enabling you to access it while offline.

- From **Internet**, tap **Tools** (three horizontal lines), tap **Add page to**, then tap **Saved pages**.

### View History

This enables you to view the recent web pages you have visited.

1. From **Internet**, tap **Tools** (three horizontal lines), then tap **History.**

2. To erase your browsing history, tap **More options** (three vertical dots), then tap **Clear History.**

**Share Pages**

This enables you to share web pages with your contacts.

- From **Internet**, tap **Tools** (three horizontal lines), then tap **share** and follow the prompts.

**Secret Mode**

Secret mode or Incognito mode enables you to surf the Internet without saving your browsing history or search history. The Secret tab has a darker shade than the normal tab windows.

1. From **Internet**, tap **Tabs** > **Turn on Secret mode.** These following options are available for added protection:
    - Smart anti-tracking.
    - Ask sites not to track me.
    - Lock Secret mode.

2. Then tap **Start**.

To disable or turn off Secret mode:

3. From Internet, tap **Tabs** > **Turn off Secret mode.**

**Internet Settings**

Modify Samsung's Internet app settings.

- From **Internet**, tap **Tools** (three horizontal lines), then tap **Settings**.

# Messages

Send text messages, emoji, and share photos using the Messages app.

- From apps, tap Messages, then Compose a new message.

**Message Search**

Quickly locate a message by using the search feature.

1. From **Messages**, tap **Search** (magnifying glass icon).

2. Enter keywords of the message you wish to find in the **Search** field, and then tap **Search** from your keyboard.

### Delete Conversations

Erase your previous conversations with this feature.

1. From **Messages**, tap ⋮ **More options** (three vertical dots), then tap **Delete**.
2. Tap on the particular conversation you wish to delete.
3. Tap **Delete** and confirm the prompts.

### Emergency Alerts

Just as the name implies, this feature notifies you of imminent danger and other situations. You don't get charged for Emergency alerts message.

1. From **Messages**, tap ⋮ **More options** (three vertical dots), tap **Settings**.
2. Then tap **Emergency alert settings** to change the notification for Emergency alerts.

### Send SOS Messages

In an emergency, use this feature to send messages with your location to your designated contacts.

1. From **Settings**, tap **Advanced features**, tap **Send SOS messages**, then toggle the switch to enable this feature.
2. Tap **Send messages to** and add recipients by selecting from your Contacts or by creating a new contact.
    - Tap **Attach pictures** to include a picture.
    - Tap **Attach audio recording** to include a five-second audio recording to your SOS message.
3. Press the side key in three quick successions to send your SOS message.

### Message Settings

Customize settings for text and multimedia messages.

- From **Messages**, tap **More options** (three vertical dots), tap **Settings**.

## My Files

View and manage files such as music, sound clips, images, and videos stored up on your Samsung Galaxy device.

- From **Apps**, tap **Samsung folder**, then tap **My files**.

4: Samsung Apps   89

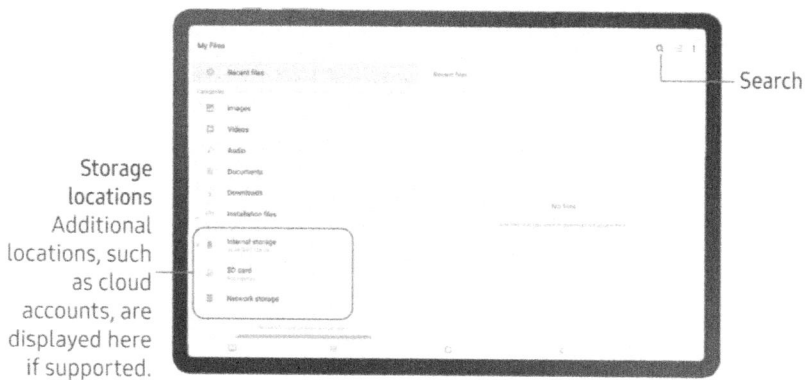

Storage locations
Additional locations, such as cloud accounts, are displayed here if supported.

Search

## File Groups

Files stored up in your Device are arranged into the following groups.

1. **Recent files:** View files you visited recently
2. **Categories:** View files based on their type or category.
3. **Storage:** View files saved in your Samsung Galaxy device, SD card, and cloud accounts.
4. **Analyze storage:** View the files that are taking up space in your storage.

## My Files Options

This tool enables you to search, Edit, clear file history, etc.

- From **My files**, these following options can be accessed:
    - **Search** (magnifying glass icon): To search and find a file or folder.

o **More options** (three vertical dots):
- **Clear Recent files list**: As the name implies, this erases the recent files list.
- **Analyze storage:** View the files that are /taking up space in your storage.
- **Trash**: Choose to either restore or permanently remove files that you have previously deleted.
- **Settings**: View your App settings.

## Phone

Use the phone app to make telephone calls and explore other advanced features.

- From your Home screen, tap **Phone.**

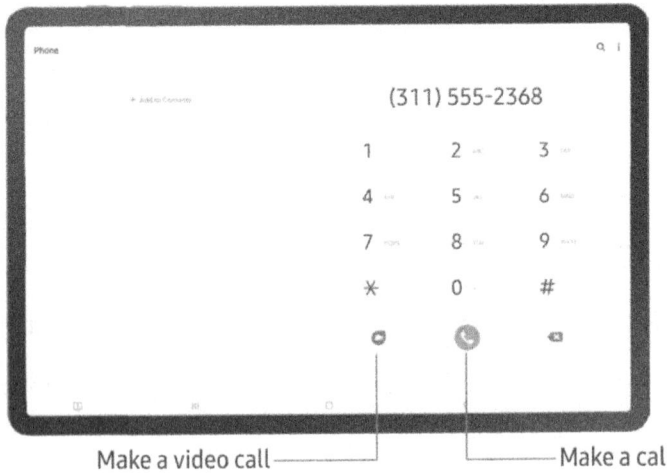
Make a video call ─── Make a call

## Calls

Use the Phone app to make calls and answer from your Home screen, Recent, Contact, etc.

### Making a Phone call

Make and answer phone calls with your Samsung Galaxy device.

- From your **Phone** app, dial a number on the keypad and tap **Call.**

### Using swipes to call

Enables this feature, and call a contact or number by swiping it to the right.

1. From **Settings**, tap **Advanced features**, tap **Motion and gestures**, then **Swipe to call or receive message**.
2. Toggle the switch to enable this feature.

### Making a call from Recent

See recent incoming, outgoing, and missed calls.

1. From the **Phone** app, tap **Recent** to see your recent calls.
2. Then tap a contact you wish to call.

### Making a call from contact

Use the Contact app to call a contact.

- From **contact**, swipe a contact to the right to call the contact.

### Answer a call

When you get an incoming call, your phone rings, and the caller's ID will be displayed. If you are on an app, a pop-up screen is displayed for the incoming call.

- On the incoming call screen, drag **answer** to the right or tap **Answer** (while on the incoming pop up screen) to answer the call.

### Decline a call

You can easily decline a call by following these quick steps:

- On the incoming call screen, drag **Decline** to the left or tap **Decline** (while on the incoming pop up screen) to decline the call.

### Decline with a message

Use this feature to decline an incoming call with a text message response.

- On the incoming call screen, drag **Send message** upward, or tap **Send message** (while on the incoming pop up screen) and select a message.

### End a call

- Tap ☎ **End** (red telephone icon) to end a call.

### Actions while on a call

While on a call, you can adjust the volume, multitask, switch to speakers or headsets.

- Press the side **volume** keys to increase or decrease the volume.

### Multitask

You can leave the call screen to use another app; the active call will be indicated on the status bar.

To get back to the call screen:

- Drag the status bar down to see the notification panel and tap **Call** to return to the call screen.

To end a call while multitasking:

- Drag the status bar down to see the notification panel and tap **End call.**

### Switch to speakers or headsets

You can listen to your calls through the loudspeakers or your Bluetooth® headset.

1. Tap **Speaker** on the call screen to listen with the loudspeakers.

2. Connect your Device via Bluetooth® to a headset to listen with the headset.

**Call pop-up settings**

Calls are displayed as pop-ups when you receive a call while using other apps.

- From the **Phone** app, tap **More options** (three vertical dots), tap **Settings**, then tap **Call display while using other apps**, and these following options are available:
    - **Fullscreen:** Use this feature to display the incoming call in full screen
    - **Pop-up:** Use this feature to display the incoming call as a pop-up at the top of your screen.
    - **Mini Pop-up:** Use this feature to display the incoming call as a pop-up.
    - **Keep calls in Pop-up:** Use this feature to keep calls in a pop-up after they are answered.

**Manage calls**

Take charge of your calls with this feature by setting up speed dials, blocking numbers, and using Voicemail.

## Call log

All the records or data of numbers you have received, dialed, or missed are stored in the Call log.

- From the **Phone** app, tap **Recent** to see your recent calls and call logs.

### Saving a number from recent calls.

Save numbers or create contacts from your recent calls.

1. From the **Phone** app, tap **Recent**
2. Select any of the recent calls you wish to save to your Contacts list, then tap **Add to account**.
3. Select either **Create new account** or **Update existing contact.**

### Delete call records

Delete any of the calls you received.

1. From the **Phone** app, tap **Recent.**
2. Long press the call you wish to delete from your Call log, then tap **Delete.**

### Block a number

You can add any number you wish to your block list. The number won't be able to reach you and will be sent directly to your Voicemail.

1. From the **Phone** app, tap **Recent.**

2. Tap the number or caller you wish to add to your block list.

3. Tap **Details(i)**, tap **Block,** and confirm the prompts.

NB: Edit and change your Blocklist in Settings. Tap **Phone**, tap **more options** icon (three vertical dots), tap **Settings**, then tap **Block numbers**.

Speed dials

Use this feature to speed dial a contact's default number by assigning a shortcut number to the contact.

1. From the **Phone** app, tap **Keyboard**, tap **More options** (three vertical dots), then tap **Speed dial numbers**. The Speed dial numbers' screen shows the speed dial numbers left or remaining.

2. Tap a number you haven't assigned.
    - Tap **Menu** to select or create a speed dial number that is different than the next one in sequence.
    - Number 1 is exclusive to Voicemail.

3. Input a number or a name, or tap **Add from Contact** to assign a contact to the speed dial number.
    - The assigned contact is displayed in the Speed dial number box.

Making a call with Speed dial

Follow these quick steps to make a call with Speed dial:

- From the **Phone** app, long-press the Speed dial number.
    - Long press the last digit if the Speed dial number is more than 1-digit long.

Removing Speed dial number

Follow these quick steps to remove an assigned Speed dial number:

1. From the **Phone** app, tap **More options** (three vertical dots), tap **Speed dial numbers.**
2. Tap **Delete**, which is by the contact you wish to remove from the Speed dial.

**Voicemail**

Access your phone's voicemail feature.

- From the **Phone** app, long-press the **number 1 key**.

**Phone settings**

This enables you to modify your Phone app settings.

- From the **Phone** app, tap **More options** (three vertical dots), then tap **Settings.**

## Optional calling services

The following services are supported if available with your service plan.

### Video calls

You have the option of making a video call.

- From the **Phone** app, dial a number on the keypad and tap **Video call.**
    - o The receiver can either answer the video call or answer it as a regular voice call.

### Place a multiparty call

This feature enables you to make another call while a call is still in progress. That is if your service plan supports it.

1. From the active call, tap **Add calls** to enter the second number for the second call.
2. Dial the second number, and then tap **call**.

When your call has been answered:

3. To switch between the two calls, tap **Swap**.
4. To hear both callers at once (multi-conferencing), tap **Merge**.

### Wi-Fi calling

Place calls with Wi-Fi when you're connected to a Wi-Fi network. Contact your carrier for details if your mobile network supports this feature.

1. From the **Phone** app, tap **More options** (three vertical dots), tap **Settings**, then tap **Wi-Fi calling**.
2. Toggle the switch to enable this feature.
3. Then follow the prompts that come along.

## Samsung notes

This app enables you to create notes containing text, images with footnote, music, and voice recordings, which can be easily shared with friends and family via social networking services.

- From your **Apps**, tap **Samsung Notes**, then tap **Create**.

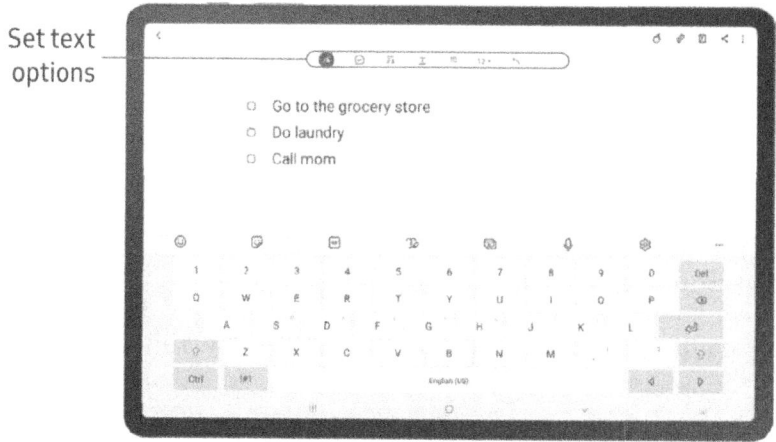

Set text options

### Create notes

Make notes with texts, images, music, and more.

1. From **Samsung Notes**, tap **Create notes** (i.e., the "plus sign" icon)
2. Tap **Save** when you're done with your note.

### Voice recordings

This feature makes it super easy to catch every word in a lecture or a very important meeting. It creates annotated voice recordings; that is, you can jot down points, questions, thoughts while recording. When you playback the recording, the note you create will correspond to the current point in your recording. This helps you keep a record of your thoughts and questions during that lecture or that very important meeting.

- From **Samsung Notes**, tap ⊕ **Create note**.
- Tap Insert (i.e., the "paper clip icon") > **Voice recordings**.
- Then create content while the audio is being recorded via the text options.

### Edit notes

Make adjustments to the notes you have created.

1. From **Samsung Notes,** tap on one of your notes to view it.
2. Tap **Edit** and make changes or adjustments.
3. Tap **More options** (i.e., the "three vertical dots icon") to access the following;
    - **Share**: Choose your file type and share the Note.
    - **Save as file**: Save the note as Samsung Note, PDF, Microsoft Word, Microsoft PowerPoint, image, or a text file.
    - **Sort pages**: Delete, cut, copy, and add pages.
    - **Page template**: Apply a template to all or some pages
    - **Background color**: Choose and apply a color to the background
    - **Add to favorites/Remove from favorites**: Add or remove notes saved to your favorite folder in the notes menu.
    - **Add tags/Edit tags**: Add tags or edit tags to search your notes easily.
    - **Finger drawing on/Finger drawing off**: Enable or disable drawing with your fingers. When it is disabled, only the S Pen can be used to draw.

4. Tap **Back** when you are done.

**Note options**

Here you have the option to edit, sort, or manage notes.

- From **Samsung Notes**, tap **More options** (three vertical dots) to access the following options:
    - **Edit**: This option enables you to share, delete, lock, or move a note.
    - **Sort**: Use this option to change the arrangement of your notes
    - **View**: Use this option to switch between Simple list, List, or Grid.

**Notes menu**

Use this feature to view your notes by category.

- From **Samsung Notes**, tap Navigation **drawer** (three horizontal lines) to access the following options:
    - **All notes**: View all the notes you have created.
    - **Frequently used notes**: Get quicker access to the notes you use regularly.
    - **Shared notebooks**: View notebooks that you have shared via Samsung account with your contacts.

- o **Trash**: View notes you have deleted for up to 15 days.
- o **Categories**: View notes by categories.
- o **Settings**: View the Settings for the Samsung Notes app.
- o **Manage categories**: Manage categories by adding, removing, and organizing the categories

## Samsung Flow

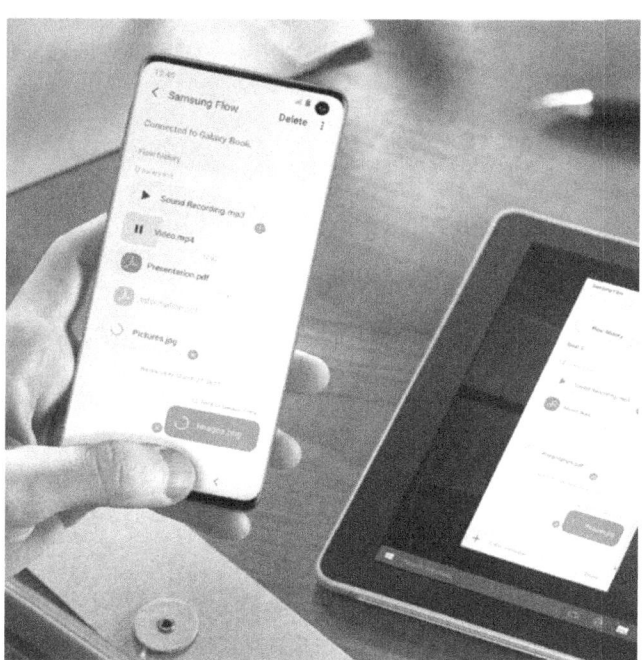

Samsung flow provides a seamless, secure, and connected experience between your smartphone and tablet. It allows you to sync notifications and reply messages, share content between devices, view smartphone content on a larger screen, etc.

The following features are available in Samsung flow:

1. **Smart View**: Share the smartphone screen on your tablet.
2. **Handover**: Transfer activity and content to a different device.
3. **Notification Sync**: Check your messages on your smartphone from your tablet and reply to it directly.
4. **Auto Hotspot Link**: Easily access the internet on your tablet via your smartphone's network connection.

To setup Samsung flow:

1. From Apps, tap **Samsung** folder, then Open **Samsung flow** on both devices
2. Choose your smartphone on the list, then confirm passcode to register the device > Set up complete.

# 5

# The Bixby

## What Is Bixby?

You might have heard Samsung users repeating these words "hi Bixby," and it seems they're having a weird conversation with their phone. Well, you are right about that!

Bixby is an intelligent virtual assistant unique and exclusive to Samsung's devices like your Galaxy S20 series, Note20 series, and Tab S7 series. It uses voice queries to answer your questions, voice commands to perform any task for you on your phone, and it also gives you recommendations by anticipating your needs and providing extrapolated reminders. Basically, anything you do via touch can be done via voice with Bixby.

## Getting Started with Bixby

It is quite easy to access Bixby on your Galaxy Tab S7 devices by simply pressing and holding the side key just beside the volume keys on the right side of your Device. After you have done that, you will be taken to Bixby home; you should then carry these mandatory steps:

1. You will get an introductory message about bringing up Bixby by pressing the side key, as I earlier stated. After all that, press next
2. Next, choose your preferred language
3. Read and accept the Terms and conditions if you agree.
4. Here you will have to sign in or sign up for a Samsung account if you don't have any.

5. Next, register your voice so Bixby can recognize your voice command

When you're done with the registration process, then you've successfully activated Bixby and can now initiate a voice command by saying "Hi Bixby" or by holding the Bixby side key on the right for it to start listening to you.

## Changing Bixby Settings

There are tons of cool adjustments you can do in the settings, which comprise of **Bixby Home**, **Bixby voice**, and **Bixby vision**. These are the settings you will find:

## Bixby Home

To get to Bixby home, you either press the Bixby side button once, or you can swipe right across your screen. You

can then access the settings by tapping the three dots at the upper right corner.

Here, you have two settings. In the first one, you have your cards, and you can select which one you want to see and the ones you want to remove when you go to Bixby home. In the second one, you can select what apps to show on the lock screen. This is not all; you can select or change the email you use for Bixby, and also, you can send location data to some apps like Uber, which will then give you contextualized data on how long to get Uber from your current location and where to check-in.

The Bixby home features are mainly your Samsung's default apps. It gives you your local weather forecast, activity stats from your Samsung's health app and can also work with Samsung's SmartThings app, giving you shortcuts to your most frequently used app, and it renders buttons to control smart locks, smart buttons, etc.

Many third-party services support the Bixby home, which helps you get quick information; as Samsung rightly put it, "a social stream for your device." Making life much more fun and a little bit easier.

## Bixby Voice: Blabbing with Bixby

It's pretty crazy what you can do with the Bixby voice. Well, you can do almost everything with it (on your mobile Device, of course, let's not get crazy). One good feature of the Bixby voice is that it's built to adapt to your manner of speech, not the other way.

You can access Bixby Voice as soon as you have downloaded and installed the software (it normally comes with your Device), completed the registering procedures, and the Bixby voice tutorial. It can then be activated by saying, "Hi Bixby" or holding the Bixby button while you talk. You can talk to Bixby like you're making a phone call, that is, if you don't want unnecessary attention (just a tip).

Bixby Voice can perform basic tasks like answering questions concerning the weather, setting alarms, setting reminders, turning on flashlight, restarting the phone, sending texts message through your Galaxy Tab S7 messaging apps, etc.

It can also handle complex tasks like writing a text or email, accept the phone call with speakers, open apps in split-screen, remind you where you parked, etc.

It also works with third-party apps like Facebook, Facebook Messenger, Instagram, WhatsApp, YouTube, Twitter, Tumblr, Expedia, Pandora, Yelp, etc. With this, Bixby has the edge over other voice assistants because it can perform multiple steps, specific commands. In more elaborate words, it can start an invoked app, go to the right screen, and complete your command. For example, Hi Bixby, Open Facebook, and post my most recent photo.

Bixby voice is customizable. You have options to select whichever voice you wish. It also has the option to include shortcuts; you can use a phrase or a word in replacement of the lengthy commands you usually use.

Samsung is improving Bixby from each update. It currently supports 3,000 commands, including the third party app commands. That's pretty impressive if you ask me!

## Bixby Vision

Have you ever seen a foreign language on the label of an item you just purchased or maybe some other thing else and you wish you could understand or translate it? This is no longer a problem with the Bixby vision, which allows you to translate a foreign language into your desired language.

You activate Bixby vision by tapping the Bixby icon in the camera app, and you can also find Bixby vision in the Gallery app, and by default, it opens in text mode. All you have to do is to get the text you want to translate into the box on your screen, and voilà! A real-time translation should appear.

Bixby vision is not limited to just translating foreign languages. Bixby vision utilizes machine learning and database partnerships, which enables it also to recognize several objects, such as food, place, image, QR codes, wine, shopping, etc.

Bixby vision tries to sort out whatever is in front of the camera and gives you information according to its findings, just like Google lens or Amazon's flow.

## Bixby Routines

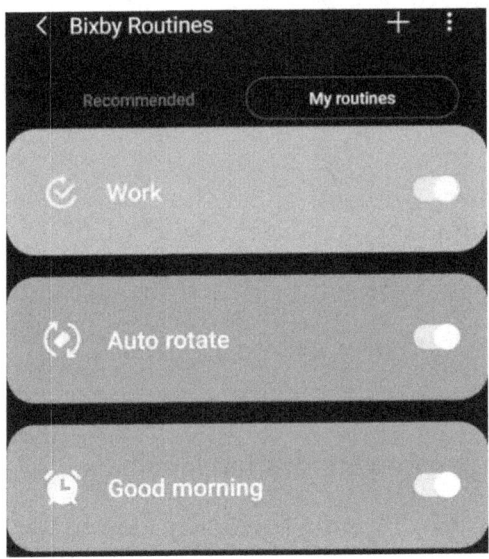

Bixby routine helps you perform often repeated tasks by learning certain triggers. It learns your routines and adapts to your life.

For example, if you connect your Galaxy device to your car Bluetooth, it'll open your Map app or Spotify and start playing a playlist. It does this by learning from your routines and giving you varieties of suggested routines that you can activate.

You can also select it manually. Maybe you always listen to Spotify when driving; you can set it to start playing whenever you connect your car Bluetooth to your Device. This is how you set up Bixby routine:

1. Open your settings and go to the advanced features.
2. Then tap the Bixby Routines switch for it to be on
3. Now that Bixby Routine is on, you can set your first routine by following these quick steps:
4. To open your options, tap Bixby Routines
5. You can either select from the preset routines or set up your new routine.
6. To set up your own routine, tap the + symbol on the top-right of your screen and complete registering your new routine

# 6

# Camera

Use the camera app to capture high-quality pictures and videos. The images and videos are stored in your Gallery, where you can view and edit them.

## Using the Galaxy Tab S7 Cameras

- To get to your camera, go to your apps and tap on camera, or you can press the power button twice if quick-launch is enabled.

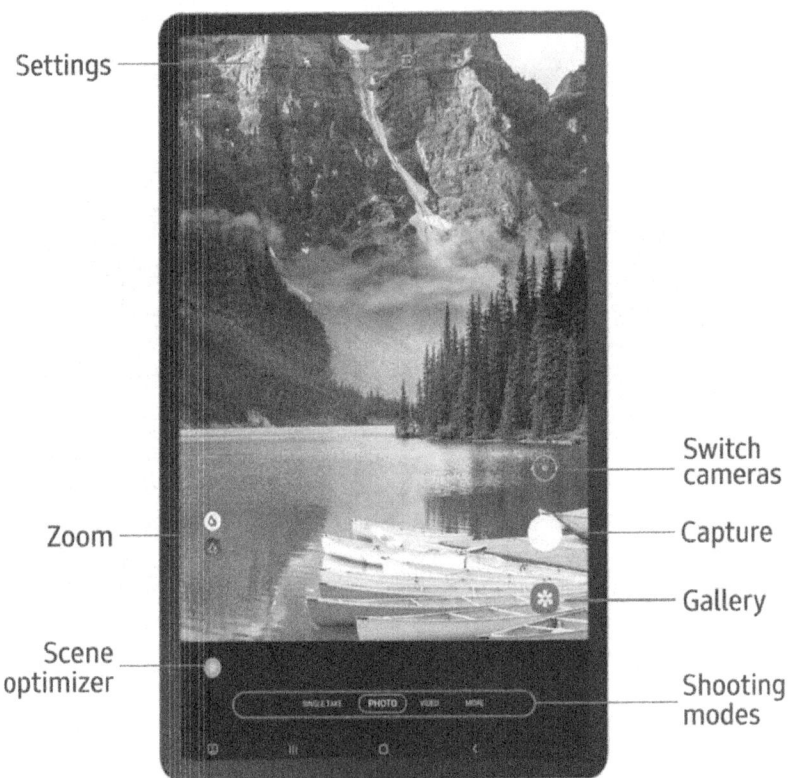

## Navigating the Camera Screen

When on the camera app, you can take pictures and navigate the screen by following these steps:

- On the camera screen, tap on what you want to focus on.
- After tapping the camera screen, a brightness scale will emerge. You can adjust the brightness by dragging the circle.
- To switch between the rear and front camera quickly, you simply swipe the camera screen up or down.
- Swipe left or right to change the shooting mode.
- Tap ◯ **capture** to take a picture.

## Configuring Your Shooting Mode

Your Galaxy Tab S7 device is automated; that is, it determines the ideal shooting mode for your picture. You can also select a shooting mode manually.

From your camera screen, swipe left to right to change the shooting mode.

- PHOTO: The camera will automatically adjust to the ideal shooting mode for the current condition.
- VIDEO: The camera will automatically adjust to the ideal shooting mode for the current condition.
- SINGLE TAKE: Capture a series of pictures and short clips of a scene by tapping on the shutter button.

**Other shooting modes**

To choose other shooting modes, tap edit and drag modes in or out of the modes tray at the bottom of your camera screen.

- PRO: This enables you to adjust the exposure value, color tone, white balance, ISO sensitivity while taking pictures
- PANORAMA: This enables you to take wide-angle shots by panning your camera across a scene.
- FOOD: This takes detailed pictures of food
- NIGHT: This mode helps you take better pictures in low light conditions without using the flash.
- PRO VIDEO: This enables you to adjust the exposure value, color tone, white balance, ISO sensitivity during video recording.
- HYPERLAPSE: This mode enables you to create your time lapse video by moving the camera around.

**AR Zone**

You can access all your Augmented Reality features from here. Go to your camera screen, swipe to more, then tap on AR Zone. You can access and use the following features in AR Zone:

- AR EMOJI CAMERA: Use this to create your Emoji Avatar.
- AR DOODLE: Use this to add line drawings and handwritings to your environment to enhance your video.
- AR EMOJI STUDIO: For creation and customization of your Emoji Avatar.
- AR EMOJI STICKERS: You use this feature to add Emoji stickers to your Emoji Avatar.
- DECO PIC: You use this to decorate real-time pictures and videos.
- HOME DECOR: Use this feature to virtually add furniture and decorations to a room to see how it will look.
- STYLING: Try on glasses using your camera

**Single Take**

This feature enables you to take both photos and videos at the same time. And with the help of AI, this shooting mode creates high-quality images and videos from multiple angles. Note that the number of images and videos created may vary.

- From your camera screen, swipe to Single Take.
- Tap on the Timer icon, and choose an option.

- Tap ○ to capture multiple angles and views by panning around the scene. All images and videos will be saved as a single entry in the Gallery.

## Live Focus

Use this feature to blur the background and have the subject on focus.

- From your camera screen, swipe to **more**, then tap live focus.
- Tap and choose the live focus effect and adjust the effect by dragging the slider.

## Scene Optimizer

This helps you to capture optimized and beautiful pictures. It does this by automatically adjusting the contrast, white balance, exposure based on what's detected by the camera.

- From the camera screen, swipe to picture and select Scene Optimizer.

NB: This feature is only available when using the rear camera.

## Recording Videos

You can record high-quality videos with your Galaxy Tab S7 devices.

- From the camera screen, swipe left to change to video shooting mode.
- Tap **Record** to start video recording.
- Tap **Capture** to take a picture while recording.
- Tap **Pause** to temporarily stop the recording, and tap **Resume** to continue your recording.
- Tap **Stop** when you're done with your recording.

### Live Focus Video

The live focus video uses the same principle with the Live focus when taking pictures. It gives you professional-looking films.

- From your camera screen, swipe to more, then tap on Live focus video.
- Tap on Live focus effect, select an effect, then adjust by dragging the slider.
- Tap capture to start your video recording.

## Camera Settings

Tap on the settings icon at the top right of your camera screen. From the settings menu, you can configure your phone's camera settings. These are the options available:

**Intelligent Features**

- SCENE OPTIMISER: This further improves the quality and effect of your images.
- SHOT SUGGESTION: This gives you suggestions and tips for the ideal shooting mode for a particular scene.
- SMART SELFIE ANGLE: Switch automatically to a wide-angle selfie for group selfies, when you want to fit everybody in or just yourself, taking your selfies to a whole new level.
- SCAN QR CODES: This detects and scans QR CODES automatically when using the camera.

**Pictures**

- SWIPE SHUTTER TO NEAREST EDGE: Select either to take a burst shot or create GIF when you swipe the shutter to the nearest edge.
- SAVING OPTIONS: Select file format and other saving options for your pictures.
    - HEIF PICTURES (PHOTO): This enables you to save pictures in high-efficiency format to save space. NB: Some sharing sites do not support this format.

- ULTRA WIDE LENS CORRECTION: This automatically fixes distortion in pictures that have been taken with Ultra-wide lens.

### Video

- REAR VIDEO SIZE: Select a resolution for your rear camera. The higher the resolution you select, the higher the quality and the bigger the memory size.
- FRONT VIDEO SIZE: Select a resolution for your front camera. The higher the resolution you select, the higher the quality and the bigger the memory size.
- HIGH EFFICIENCY VIDEO: This enables you to record videos in high-efficiency format to save space. NB: Some sharing sites and some devices do not support this format.
- VIDEO STABILIZATION: Activate to remove unwanted camera shakes and jitters.

## Useful Features

- AUTO HDR: This helps you to capture more details of the bright and dark areas of your pictures.
- SELFIE TONE: Add shade or varieties of color to your selfies.

- PICTURES AS PREVIEWED: This saves pictures exactly how you previewed them on the camera screen without flipping.
- GRID LINES: It enables you to apply the rule of thirds for better positioning of objects in an image.
- LOCATION TAG: This adds your GPS location tag to your picture.
- SHOOTING METHODS:
    - PRESS VOLUME KEY TO: Enable you to use the volume key to control system volume, zoom, and take videos and pictures.
    - FLOATING SHUTTER BUTTON: Add a second shutter button that you can move anywhere on your camera screen.
    - SHOW PALM: Enables you to take pictures by placing your palm in front of your camera screen.
- STORAGE LOCATION: Select where to store your pictures and videos
- SHUTTER SOUND: Make a sound when taking a picture.
- RESET SETTINGS: Reset your camera settings.

- ABOUT CAMERA: View the camera app and your software details or information.

# 7

# Gallery

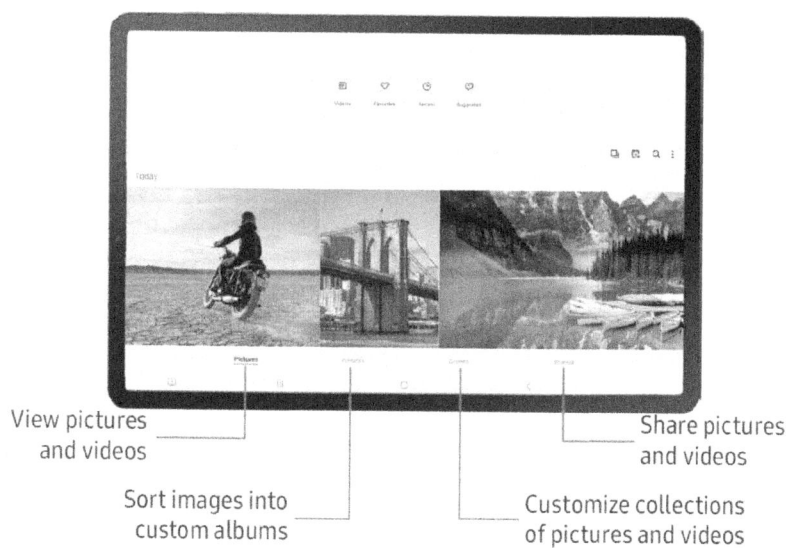

View pictures and videos

Sort images into custom albums

Share pictures and videos

Customize collections of pictures and videos

The gallery app is a simple tool that enables you to view all the visual media (pictures and videos) stored up on your Mobile Device. The app allows you to view, edit, and manage your pictures and videos stored on your Samsung Galaxy Tab S7 device.

- From your app, tap **Gallery**.

## View pictures

The pictures that you have taken and stored on your Device are viewable in the Samsung gallery app.

1. From your Gallery, tap on pictures.
2. Tap on a picture to view that particular picture, swipe left or right to view the next and previous pictures.
   - To mark the current picture as your favorite, tap the heart icon
   - To access these following features tap on more options.
     - **Details:** View and edit the information about your picture.
     - **Set as wallpaper:** To set the current picture as your wallpaper.
     - **Send as live image:** Draw an animation with live image on a picture and share it
     - **Move to secure folder:** To move the picture to a secure folder.
     - **Print:** To send the picture to a connected printer.

# Edit pictures

Perfect your pictures by using this tool in your gallery.

1. From your Device's Gallery, tap on pictures.
2. View the picture by tapping on it, then tap the pencil (Edit) icon, and these options will be available:
    - **Transform:** Use this option to rotate, crop, flip, and make other changes to the appearance of your picture.
    - **Filters:** Use this option to add color effects
    - **Tone:** Use this option to alter contrast, brightness, exposure, etc.
    - **Sticker:** Use this option to overlay animated stickers.
    - **Text:** Use this option to add texts to your picture
    - **Draw:** Use this option to add handwritten or hand-drawn content.
    - **Auto adjust:** Use this option to apply to automatic adjustments to improve the picture.
    - **Reset:** Use this option to restore the original picture by undoing the changes applied.
3. When done, save the new changes.

## View videos

The videos you have stored up on your mobile Device are viewable in your Samsung Gallery app. You can save videos as your favorites and can also view the video details.

1. From your Gallery, tap on pictures.
2. Tap on a video to view that particular video, swipe left or right to view the next and previous.
    - To create your favorite album tab, tap favorite (heart icon), and the video is added to the album.
    - To access these following features tap on more options.
        - **Details:** View and edit the information about your video.
        - **Send as live image:** Draw an animation with live image on a video and share it.
        - **Move to secure folder:** To move the picture to a secure folder.
3. Tap the play icon to play the current video.

## Video enhancer

Enable this feature to enhance the overall look of videos to enjoy brighter and more vivid colors (Galaxy Tab S7+ only).

1. Go to your device settings, tap on advanced features.
2. Tap on video enhancer.
3. Toggle the switch to enable this feature.

## Edit videos

1. From your Gallery app, tap on pictures.
2. Tap on a video to view it.
3. Tap **Edit** (pencil icon) to access the following tools:
    - **Rotate:** Use this tool to rotate the video clockwise
    - **Trim:** Cut segments of your video and trim to the desired length
    - **Filters:** Use this tool to add visual effects to your videos
    - **Portrait:** This tool enhances facial features like skin tones, eye, etc.
    - **Text:** Use this tool to add text to your videos.
    - **Sticker:** Use this tool to overlay animated stickers.
    - **Draw:** Use this option to add handwritten or hand-drawn content to your video.

- **Speed:** Alter the play speed.
- **Audio:** Adjust the video's volume and insert the music background to the video.

4. Save your new changes and confirm the prompt.

## Share pictures and videos

Share your pictures and videos using your Gallery app.

1. From your Gallery app, tap pictures.
2. Tap **More options**, tap **share**, then tap on the pictures and videos you wish to share.
3. Tap **Share**, and select the app or the means you want to use to share the pictures and videos. Follow the message prompt

## Delete pictures and videos

Delete unwanted pictures and videos stored on your device.

1. From your Gallery app, tap on more options, tap on Edit.
2. Tap on and select the pictures and videos you wish to delete or tap the **Select All** checkbox at the top of the screen if you wish to select everything.
3. Tap on Delete and confirm the prompt.

## Create a movie

Make a film on your Device and share it with family and friends from your Gallery App. Create a slideshow with music and video effect.

1. From your Gallery app, tap **Create movie**.
2. Select the pictures and videos you want in your movie
3. Tap on **Create movie**, then choose from these two options: **Highlight reel** (automatic slideshow) or **Self-edited** (custom slideshow). The following tools are available.
    - **Duration:** Adjust the run-time of your movie (**Highlight reel** only).
    - **Transition effect:** Customize the transition between each clip by adding visual interest to your movie (**self-edited** only)
    - **Title:** Add the title and description of your movie.
    - **Audio:** Adjust the volume level of your movie, add music or sound effects.
    - **Clips:** View and edit each selected pictures and videos in your movie.
    - **Add:** Include additional clips from your Gallery app (**self-edited** only).
    - **Share:** Send the movie to friends and family.

4. Tap save to save the movie.

## Take a Screenshot

Capture the current image on your screen. Your Screenshot album will be created automatically in the Gallery app.

- Press and release the side and volume down keys to take a screenshot of your current screen.

**Use Palm Swipe to Capture a Screenshot**

1. Go to your device settings, tap on **advanced features**, select **motion and gestures > palm swipe to capture**.
2. Toggle the switch to enable this feature.

**Screenshot Settings**

Change the screenshot and screen recorder settings.

- Go to your device settings, tap on advanced features, select screenshot, and screen recorder.
    - **Screenshot toolbar:** Show more options after you take a screenshot.
    - **Delete shared screenshots:** To delete screenshot automatically after they are shared via the screenshot toolbar.

- **Screenshot format:** Select to save your screenshots as either JPG or PNG files.

## Screen Recorder

Record the activities on your screen and share them with family and friends.

1. Go to Quick settings (by swiping down from the top of your screen), tap on screen recorder to start your recording.
   - Tap the pencil icon to draw on the screen
   - Tap selfie video to use your front camera and include the recording.
2. Tap stop when done with your recording. Your recording will be saved to the screen recording album in your Gallery app automatically.

### Screen Recorder Settings

Select the quality and sound settings for your screen recorder.

1. Go to your device settings, tap on **advanced features**, select **screenshot and screen recorder > screen recorder settings**.
   - **Sounds:** Choose the sounds you want your screen recorder to record.

- **Video quality:** Select the quality and resolution. Higher the resolution, the higher the quality and the higher the memory required.
- **Selfie video size**: Drag the slider to adjust the size of your video overlay.

# 8

# Display

You can adjust the screen display settings to fit your preference. The Galaxy Tab S7 has one of the finest displays in the cell phone industry right now. Unlike the traditional 60Hz refresh rate found in lower models and other phone brands, the Galaxy Tab S7 comes with a Dynamic AMOLED Infinity-O display with up to 120Hz refresh rate, thereby giving it the smoothest and highest-frame-rate display ever.

Unlike the Samsung flagship phones, where you'd have to sacrifice the native 1440p/WQHD+ resolution for a lower 1080p/FHD+ resolution to use the 120Hz display, the Galaxy Tab S7 makes it possible for you to use the WQHD+ with the high 120Hz refresh rate. This improvement, no doubt, make this device to have the finest displays in the cell phone industry, as earlier stated.

## Motion Smoothness

Increase the screen's refresh rate to get more realistic animations and smoother scrolling. You can either select **120Hz** or **Standard** that is at 60Hz.

1. From **Settings**, tap **Display menu**.
2. From the display menu list, tap **Motion smoothness**, then select an option and tap apply

## Screen Resolution

Out of the box, your Samsung Galaxy Tab S7 is set to FHD+. You can increase it to WQHD+ to sharpen image quality.

1. From **Settings**, tap **Display menu**.
2. From the display menu list, tap **Screen resolution**.
3. Your choices are HD+ (1,600 x 720), FHD+ (2,400 x 1,080), and WQHD+ (3,200 x 1,440).
4. Select your preferred screen resolution, then tap **Apply**.

TIPS: To get the best out of your Samsung Tab, the WQHD+ screen resolution – alongside the 120Hz display – is the preferred choice.

Some apps may not support lower or higher screen resolution settings and may not open when you change the resolution.

## Dark Mode

Utilize this feature and switch to a darker theme to keep your eyes more comfortable at night.

- From **Settings**, tap **Display menu** and select from the following options:
    - **Light**: This is your default theme. It applies a light color theme to your device.
    - **Dark**: This applies a dark color theme to your device.
    - **Dark mode settings**: This feature allows you to customize where and when dark mode is applied or utilized.
        - **Turn on as scheduled**: Configure **dark mode** for either **Custom schedule** or **Sunset to sunrise**.
        - **Apply to wallpaper**: This Applies the dark mode settings to the wallpaper.
        - **Adaptive color filter**: This feature helps in reducing eye strain by turning on the blue light filter automatically between sunset and sunrise (For Galaxy Tab S7 only).

## Screen Brightness

Use this feature to adjust your device's screen brightness according to personal preference or lighting conditions.

1. From **Settings**, tap **Display menu**.
2. Customize your device's screen brightness with these two features:
    - Tap **Adaptive brightness** to allow your device to adjust the screen brightness according to lighting conditions automatically.
    - Or drag the **Brightness** slider to set the screen brightness to your personal preference manually.

TIPS: You can also customize your screen brightness to preference from the **Quick settings** panel.

## Blue Light Filter

This feature reduces the amount of blue light displayed on your device's screen. Blue light can suppress melatonin (sleep-inducing hormone) production, so this feature makes sleeping better.

- From **Settings**, tap **Display menu** > **Blue light filter**, then choose from one of the following options:

- Drag the **Opacity** slider to set the opacity of the filter to your personal preference.
- Tap **Turn on now** to enable the blue light filter.
- Tap **Turn on as scheduled** to set a schedule when the blue light filter should be enabled. You can choose either **Sunset to sunrise** or **Custom schedule**.

## Screen Mode

This feature modifies how saturated or vivid the colors on your screen will be. You can adjust the display color to your preference or just select a screen mode suitable for your current activity.

1. From **Settings**, tap **Display** > **Screen mode**.
2. Tap one of the following options to set a different screen mode.

## Font Size and Style

Use this feature to customize your device's font size and style.

- From **Settings**, tap **Display** > **Font size and style** to access the following options:
    - Tap **Font style** and choose a different font.

- Tap a font to select it or tap **download fonts** to download and add fonts from the Galaxy.
  o Tap **Bold font** to apply it to your font.
  o Drag the **Font size** slider to adjust the text size to your preference.

## Screen Zoom

Increase or decrease the size of the content on the screen by adjusting the zoom level.

1. From **Settings**, tap **Display** > **Screen zoom**.
2. Drag the **Screen zoom** slider to adjust the zoom level to your preference.

TIP: This feature can be useful to older adults or anyone with eye defects.

## Screen Timeout

Use this feature to set the screen to turn off after a set amount of time of inactivity.

- From **Settings**, tap **Display menu** > **Screen timeout**, then tap and select a time limit.

TIP: Always turn off the display screen when not in use to save battery life and also avoid degradation of image quality.

## Accidental Touch Protection

Use this feature to prevent accidental operation caused by fabric sliding or extrusion when the device is in a pocket or bag.

- From **Settings**, tap **Display menu** > **Accidental touch protection** to enable or disable this feature.

## Show Charging Information

This feature allows you to view the battery life and the estimated time it will take for your device to be fully charged while the screen is turned off.

- From **Settings**, tap **Display** > **Show charging information** to enable this feature.

## Screen Saver

This feature allows you to display photos or colors when the screen is turned off or while charging.

1. From **Settings**, tap **Display menu** > **Screen saver**.
2. Then choose one of the following options:
    - **None**: To not display a screen saver.
    - **Colors**: Select this to display a changing screen of colors.

- **Photo table**: Select this to display pictures in a photo table.
- **Photo frame**: Select this to display pictures in a photo frame.
- **Photos:** Select this to display pictures from your google photos account.

3. Tap **Preview** for a demonstration of your selected screen saver.

TIP: For additional options, tap **Settings** next to a feature.

## Reduce Animations

Enable this feature to reduce certain motion effects, such as when you open or close an app.

- From **Settings**, tap **Advanced features** > **Reduce animations** to enable this feature.

## Double-tap to Wake

Turn on your device's screen by double-tapping the screen instead of pressing the side key.

- From **Settings**, tap **Advanced features** > **Motion and gestures** > **Double tap to wake** to enable this feature.

## Smart Stay

This cool feature uses your front camera to detect your face so that the screen stays on while you are looking at it.

- From **Settings**, tap **Advanced features** > **Motion and gestures** > **Smart stay**, then toggle the switch to enable this feature.

# 9

# Connections

Take charge of the connections between your Samsung Galaxy device and other devices and networks.

Wi-Fi | Bluetooth | Airplane mode | Mobile networks | Data usage | Mobile hotspot | Tethering | Nearby device scanning | Connect to a printer | Virtual Private Networks | Private DNS | Ethernet

## Wi-Fi

Access the internet without using your mobile data by connecting your Samsung Galaxy device to a Wi-Fi network.

1. From **Settings**, tap **Connections**, tap **Wi-Fi**, then toggle the switch to turn on Wi-Fi and scan for available networks.
2. Tap a network, enter a password if demanded.

**Manually connect to a Wi-Fi network**

You can opt to connect manually to a Wi-Fi network if the Wi-Fi network you want is not found after a scan. Before you start, ask the Wi-Fi network administrator for the name and password.

1. From **Settings**, tap **Connections**, tap **Wi-Fi**, then toggle the switch to turn on Wi-Fi.
2. Tap **Add network**, which is at the bottom of the list.
3. Enter the Wi-Fi network information:
    - **Network name**: Type the name of the network.
    - **Security**: From the list, select a security option and enter a password if required.
    - **MAC address type**: Choose the type of MAC address to use for the connection.
    - **Auto reconnect**: This option enables you to automatically reconnect to the Wi-Fi network whenever you are in range.
    - **Advanced**: Add advanced options, such as Proxy settings, IP.
4. Tap **Save**.

**Advanced Wi-Fi settings**

Use the Advanced Wi-Fi settings feature to configure connections to various Hotspots and Wi-Fi networks and check your Samsung Galaxy device's network addresses and manage your saved networks.

1. From **Settings**, tap **Connections**, tap **Wi-Fi**, then toggle the switch to turn on Wi-Fi.
2. Tap **More options** (three vertical dots), then tap **Advanced**.
    - **Switch to mobile data**: This enables your device to automatically switch to mobile data whenever the connection to your Wi-Fi network is weak or unstable and to switch back to your Wi-Fi network when it gets stable.
    - **Turn on Wi-Fi automatically**: This turns on your Wi-Fi network when you go close to wireless routers you frequently use.
    - **Detect suspicious networks**: This notifies you of any suspicious activity on your Wi-Fi network.
    - **Wi-Fi power saving mode**: Reduce battery usage by enabling Wi-Fi traffic analysis.

- **Network notification**: This notifies you whenever it detects an open network in range.
- **Manage networks**: This enables you to view your saved networks and configure whether to auto-reconnect or forget individual networks.
- **Wi-Fi control history**: This lets you view apps that have turned on/off your Wi-Fi network recently.
- **Hotspot 2.0**: This allows you to connect automatically to Wi-Fi networks that support Hotspot 2.0.
- **Install network certificates**: Install your network authentication certificates.
- **MAC address**: View your Samsung Galaxy device's MAC address, which is mandatory when connecting to some secured networks (It is not configurable).
- **IP address**: View your Samsung Galaxy device's IP address (it is not configurable).

**Wi-Fi Direct**

Use Wi-Fi direct to share data between devices by establishing a direct, peer to peer Wi-Fi connection without requiring a wireless router.

1. From **Settings**, tap **Connections**, tap **Wi-Fi**, then toggle the switch to turn on Wi-Fi.
2. Tap **More options** (three vertical dots), then tap **Wi-Fi Direct**.
3. Tap and select a device and follow the prompts to connect.

TIPS: You can use this feature when sharing a file by tapping **Wi-Fi Direct.**

**Disconnect from Wi-Fi Direct**

Terminate connection between your Samsung Galaxy device and a Direct Wi-Fi device.

1. From **Settings**, tap **Connections**, tap **Wi-Fi**.
2. Tap **More options** (three vertical dots), tap **Wi-Fi Direct**, then tap a device to disconnect it.

# Bluetooth

This feature enables you to pair your Samsung Galaxy device to other Bluetooth enabled devices, like Bluetooth headphones, AirPods, or Bluetooth in-car infotainment systems. Once you have successfully paired the devices, the devices will remember each other and can share information without entering the passkey again.

1. From **Settings**, tap **Connections**, tap **Bluetooth,** then toggle the switch to turn on Bluetooth.

2. Tap a device and follow the prompts to connect to the device.

### Renaming a Paired Device

Rename your paired device for easier recognition.

1. From **Settings**, tap **Connections**, tap **Bluetooth,** then toggle the switch to turn on Bluetooth.
2. Tap the **Settings** icon next to the device name, then tap **Rename**.
3. Enter a new device name and tap **Rename**.

### Unpair from a Bluetooth Device

Unpair from a Bluetooth device if you no longer want your Samsung Galaxy device and the Bluetooth device to recognize each other.

1. From **Settings**, tap **Connections**, tap **Bluetooth,** then toggle the switch to turn on Bluetooth.
2. Tap the **Settings** icon next to the device name, then tap **Unpair**.

**TIP:** If, by any chance, you want to connect to the Bluetooth device, you will need to pair again with it.

### Advanced Options

Access additional Bluetooth features in the Advanced menu.

1. From **Settings**, tap **Connections**, tap **Bluetooth**.
2. Tap Advanced to access the following:
    - **Music share**: This feature makes it possible for your friends to play music through your headphones or Bluetooth speakers without having to set up a connection with their device and your headphone or Bluetooth speaker. Instead, your Samsung Galaxy device act as a conduit for the connection.
    - **Ringtone sync**: This enables you to use the ringtone set on your Samsung Galaxy device when you receive calls through a connected Bluetooth device.
    - **Bluetooth control history**: View apps that have made use of Bluetooth recently.

**Dual Audio**

This feature enables you to play music or audio from your Samsung Galaxy device to two connected Bluetooth audio devices.

1. Connect the Bluetooth audio devices to your Samsung Galaxy device.
2. Tap ⏵ **Media** from the notification panel.
3. Under audio output, tap the **tick** icon next to each audio device to play music or audio to them.

## Airplane Mode

Turn off connectivity features and disconnect your Samsung Galaxy device from all networks by enabling Airplane mode.

1. From **Settings**, tap **Connections** > **Airplane mode**.
2. Then toggle the switch to enable this feature.

## Mobile networks

Use Mobile networks to configure your Samsung Galaxy device's ability to connect to mobile networks and use mobile data.

- From **Settings**, tap **Connections** > **Mobile networks**.
    - o **Data roaming**: This feature allows your Samsung Galaxy device to connect to a mobile network while traveling outside your carrier's network territory.
    - o **Network mode**: Select the Network mode you want your Samsung Galaxy device to use.
    - o **Access Point Names**: Choose or add your Access Point Names (APNs), which have the network settings to connect your Samsung Galaxy device to your provider.

o **Network operators**: Choose available and your preferred networks.

## Data Usage

This feature allows you to check your current Wi-Fi and mobile data consumption or usage. It also allows you to customize warnings and limits.

From **Settings**, tap **Connections** > **Data usage**

### Turn on Data Saver

Turning on Data saver cuts down your data consumption by restricting selected apps from sending and receiving data in the background.

1. From **Settings**, tap **Connections** > **Data usage**, then tap **Data saver**.
2. Tap or toggle the switch to turn on **Data saver**.
   - o To grant some apps unrestricted usage, tap **Allow app while Data saver is on** and tap or toggle the switch next to each app.

### Monitor Mobile Data

Set limits and restrictions to customize your mobile data access.

- From **Settings**, tap **Connections** > **Data usage.** These following options are available:

- **Mobile data**: Make use of your mobile data plan.
- **Mobile data only apps**: Set apps to always use mobile data, even when your Samsung Galaxy device is connected to a Wi-Fi network.
- **Mobile data usage**: View your mobile data usage over a period of time. You can view the overall usage as well as the specific usage by each app.
- **Billing cycle and data warning**: You can reset and change the monthly date to match your carrier's billing date.

TIP: Make use of these features to manage and optimize your data usage.

**Monitor Wi-Fi Data**

Customize usage limits and networks to restrict Wi-Fi data access.

1. From **Settings**, tap **Connections** > **Data usage**.
2. Tap **Wi-Fi data usage** to view your Wi-Fi data usage over a period of time. You can view the overall usage as well as the specific usage by each app.

## Mobile Hotspot

A mobile hotspot enables you to create a Wi-Fi network with your data plan that can be used by multiple devices.

1. From **Settings**, tap **Connections** > **Mobile hotspot and tethering,** then tap **Mobile hotspot**.
2. Toggle the switch to turn on your Mobile hotspot.
3. On the devices you want to connect, turn on their Wi-Fi, and select your device's Mobile hotspot, then enter the Mobile hotspot password to connect.
    - Tap **Connected devices** to view the number of devices that are connected to your Mobile hotspot.

### Change the Mobile Hotspot Password

Change your default Mobile hotspot password to a customized one that is easier to recall.

1. From **Settings**, tap **Connections** > **Mobile hotspot and tethering,** then tap **Mobile hotspot**.
2. Tap **Password**, enter a new password, then tap **Save**.

### Configuring the Mobile Hotspot Settings

You can customize your Mobile hotspot settings to your preferred specifications.

1. From **Settings**, tap **Connections** > **Mobile hotspot and tethering,** then tap **Mobile hotspot**.

2. Tap **More options** (three vertical dots), then tap **Configure mobile hotspot** to access the following setting:
    - **Network name**: Use this feature to view and also to change your Mobile hotspot name.
    - **Broadcast network name (SSID)**: Make the hotspot of your Samsung Galaxy device visible to others.
    - **Security**: Select the level of security for your Mobile hotspot.
    - **Password**: If you selected a security level that demands a password, you could view and change the password.
    - **Maximum connections**: Select the maximum number of devices that can connect to your Mobile hotspot at once.
    - **Power saving mode**: Optimize your battery by analyzing hotspot traffic.
    - **Timeout settings**: Select how long to allow devices to remain idle while connected to the Mobile hotspot.
    - **Protected management frames**: This feature gives you additional privacy protection.

### Wi-Fi Sharing

This feature allows you to share your Wi-Fi network with other devices without giving out your Wi-Fi password.

1. From **Settings**, tap **Connections** > **Mobile hotspot and tethering**, then tap **Mobile hotspot**.
2. Tap **More options** (three vertical dots), then tap **Wi-Fi sharing** to turn on this feature.

### Band

Select one of the bandwidth options.

- From **Settings**, tap **Connections** > **Mobile hotspot and tethering**, then tap **Mobile hotspot**.
- Tap **Band** and select an option.

### Auto Hotspot

This feature allows you to share your Mobile hotspot with other devices signed in to your Samsung account.

1. From **Settings**, tap **Connections** > **Mobile hotspot and tethering**, then tap **Mobile hotspot**.
2. Tap **Auto hotspot**, and toggle the switch to enable this feature.

## Tethering

Tethering or Phone-as-modem allows you to share your device's internet with other connected computers.

1. From **Settings**, tap **Connections** > **Mobile hotspot and tethering,** then tap **Mobile hotspot**.
2. Connect the computer to your Samsung Galaxy device via USB cable, then tap **USB tethering**
3. You can also opt for wireless LAN over Bluetooth by tapping **Bluetooth tethering**.

## Nearby Device Scanning

This feature lets you know if there are devices nearby that you can connect to. It uses Bluetooth Low Energy, so it stays on even after you turn off the Bluetooth.

1. From **Settings**, tap **Connections** > **More connection settings**, tap **Nearby device scanning**.
2. Toggle the switch to enable this feature.

## Connect to a Printer

This feature allows you to connect your Samsung Galaxy device to a printer on the same Wi-Fi network, thereby enabling easy printing of documents from your Samsung Galaxy device.

1. From **Settings**, tap **Connections** > **More connection settings**, tap **Printing**.

2. Tap **Download plugin**, follow the prompts and add a print service.

3. Tap the print service, and tap **More options** (three vertical dots), then tap **Add printer**.

## Virtual Private Networks

From your Samsung Galaxy device, connect to a private secured network by using a Virtual Private Network (VPN). Get the connection information from your VPN administrator before you begin.

1. From **Settings**, tap **Connections** > **More connection settings**, tap **VPN**.

2. Tap **More options** (i.e., the "three vertical dots"), then tap **Add VPN profile**.

3. Enter the VPN connection information given to you by your network administrator and then tap **Save**.

### Managing a VPN

Edit or delete a VPN connection from the VPN settings menu.

1. From **Settings**, tap **Connections** > **More connection settings**, tap **VPN**.

2. Tap **Settings** next to the VPN you wish to edit or delete.

3. Tap **Edit** to edit the VPN and tap **Save** when you're done, or tap **Delete** to remove the VPN.

**Connecting to a VPN**

After you have set up a VPN, connecting and disconnecting from the VPN is quite easy.

1. From **Settings**, tap **Connections** > **More connection settings**, tap **VPN**.
2. Tap a **VPN**, enter your login details, and tap **Connect**.
    - While to disconnect, tap the **VPN**, and then tap **Disconnect**.

## Private DNS

Connect your Samsung Galaxy device to a private DNS host.

1. From **Settings**, tap **Connections** > **More connection settings**, tap **Private DNS**.
2. Choose one of the available options to configure a private DNS connection, then tap **Save**.

## Ethernet

Use Ethernet cable to connect your Samsung Galaxy device to a local network if the wireless connection is down.

1. Connect an Ethernet cable to your Samsung Galaxy device.

2. From **Settings**, tap **Connections** > **More connection settings**, tap **Ethernet**, and then follow the prompts.

**TIP:** An adapter will be needed to connect the Ethernet cable to your Samsung Galaxy device.

# 10

# Other Cool Features

Access other cool features like the Samsung Dex, Edge Screen, xCloud, etc.

## Samsung DeX

The word "Dex" is a contraction of these two words, "Desktop Experience." So, Samsung Dex is a feature that enables you to use your device like a PC by connecting the device to an external display such as your TV or Computer.

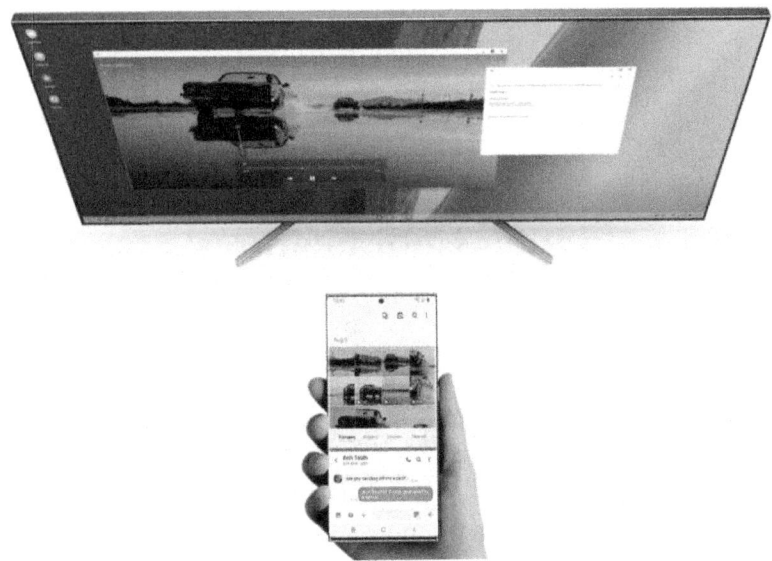

Unlike its predecessors, Samsung Galaxy Tab S7 doesn't require accessories like a USB cable, DeX Station, DeX Pad to connect the devices. Your Samsung Galaxy device provides Wireless DeX that allows you to connect to a Smart TV or PC via Wi-Fi. It gives you an exhilarating multitasking experience on a large screen. You can operate separate apps on the external display and your device simultaneously. That is, you can watch online lectures on the TV while taking notes with the Samsung Notes, or you can surf the Web with the device while watching Netflix or YouTube with the TV.

- From any screen, swipe down to open Quick settings, then tap **DeX**.

- Select your TV from the detected devices list, then tap **Start now** on the Samsung DeX pop-up (required for devices after Android 10 (Q OS)
- Accept the TV's connection request, and the Samsung DeX will appear on the TV when they connect.
- To switch to Touch Pad, after connecting to DeX, swipe down the Quick settings and tap **Run with Touch Pad**.
- With three of your fingers, do a swipe-up gesture on your device screen to go back to Recent page, swipe down to go to Home, swipe left/right to switch apps.

Note

- Samsung Wireless DeX is only supported by Smart TVs that support Miracast.
- Screen Mirroring must be supported on the TV you want to connect to.
- Samsung recommends using Samsung Smart TV manufactured after 2019.
- You can operate up to five apps simultaneously on the TV via DeX mode.
- You must download the Dex app on to your computer at **Samsungdex.com** to connect to your PC.

## Microsoft apps

Enjoy these four apps: Outlook, LinkedIn, Office, and OneDrive from Microsoft.

### Outlook

This gives you access to contacts, emails, tasks, calendar, etc.

- Go to **Apps**, then tap **Microsoft** folder > **Outlook**.

### LinkedIn

Connect and network with other career and business professionals around the world.

### Office

This allows you to enjoy access to Word, Excel, and PowerPoint app on your mobile device.

### OneDrive

This app allows you to store and share documents, photos, and videos in your free online OneDrive account, which you can access with your personal computer, tablet, or phone.

## Edge screen

The Edge screen consists of a customizable Edge panel and Edge lighting. The Edge panel gives you easy access to your contacts, apps, tasks, as well as viewing news, sports, etc.

10: Other Cool Features   169

Edge handle

**Configure Edge panels**

The edge panels are customizable.

1. Swipe left on the Edge handle to open the menu, tap  **Settings**.
2. Toggle the switch to enable the feature. The following options are available:
   - **Check box**: Select or deselect each panel.
   - **Edit** (if available): Customize individual panels.
   - **Search**: Look for panels that are either installed or available to install.
   - **More options**
     - **Reorder**: Drag the panels to the left or to the right to change their order.

- **Uninstall**: Delete an installed edge panel from your device.
- **Handle settings**: Configure the style and position of the Edge handle.
- **Contact us**: Contact Samsung support via Samsung Members
  - **Galaxy store**: Search for and download additional Edge panels.
3. Tap ⟨ **Back** to save current changes.

**Edge panel position**

Change the position of the Edge handle to your preference.

1. Swipe left on the Edge handle to open the menu, tap ⚙ **Settings**.
2. Tap ⋮ **More option** > **Handle Settings** for the following:
   - **Edge handle**: Drag to adjust the position of the Edge handle along the edge of the screen.
   - **Position**: Choose the side the Edge screen display on, either left or right.
   - **Lock handle position**: Enable this to prevent the handle position from being moved when touched and held.

**Edge panel style**

Customize the Edge panel style.

1. Swipe left on the Edge handle to open the menu, tap ⚙ **Settings**.

2. Tap ⋮ **More option** > **Handle Settings** for the following:

    o **Color**: Select a color for the Edge handle.

    o **Transparency**: Adjust the transparency of the Edge handle by dragging the slider.

    o **Size**: Adjust the size of the Edge handle by dragging the slider.

**Apps panel**

You can add a maximum of ten apps in two columns to the Apps panel.

1. From any screen, drag the **Edge handle** to the center of your screen, swipe until the **Apps panel** appears.

2. Tap an app to open it or tap **Edit panel** to add more apps to the Apps panel.

## Multi Window

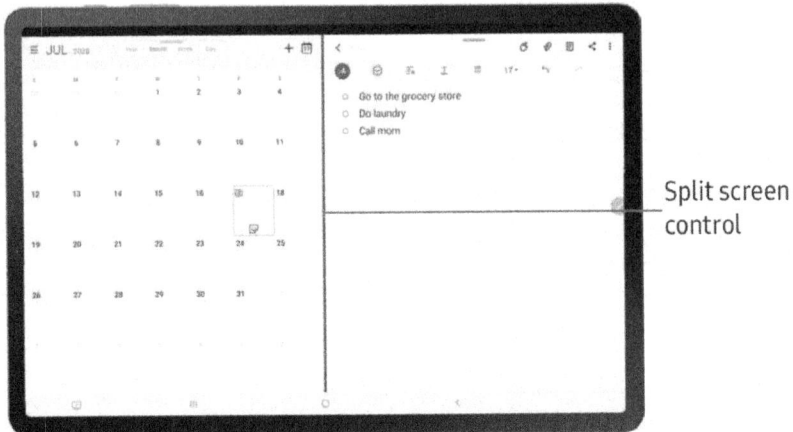

This feature gives you the ability to multitask by opening several apps on your tablet simultaneously. It only works on apps that support split screen. You can switch between these apps and adjust the size of their windows as deemed fit.

To use this feature:

1. Tap ||| Recent apps (located at the bottom left of the screen) from any screen.
2. To open an app in split screen, tap the app icon and select **Open in split screen view**.
3. To add another app to the split screen view, tap on the app icon in the other window. To adjust the window size, drag the middle of the window border to the left or right (down or up).

## Window Controls

The window controls help you adjust the looks of apps that are opened in the split screen view.

1. Drag the middle of the window border to adjust the size of the windows.
2. Tap the middle of the window border for the following options.

    - ▭ **Split horizontally**: When holding your tablet vertically, then you can view the windows horizontally. When holding your tablet in a horizontal position, this option will change to **Split vertically.**
    - ⇄ **Switch Windows**: Swap the two windows to interchange their position.
    - ⊞ **Add app combo to Edge screen**: Create and add your most frequently used app pair shortcut to the app panel on the edge screen.

## xCloud- Xbox game streaming

At the Galaxy unpacked event, Samsung announced that it is partnering with Xbox to bring Xbox game pass ultimate to the Samsung Galaxy Devices.

This simply means, starting from September 15$^{th}$, 2020, project xCloud (Xbox's cloud-gaming service) will be added to the Xbox game pass ultimate at no cost, although it comes with a subscription fee. This gives you free access to more than 100 console games, thereby giving you the best mobile gaming experience available.

# About the Author

Dylan Blake and Patrick Garner are two Tech enthusiasts or technomaniacs who like to explore the technological world and demystify her mysteries. They both have been in this field for more than ten years and are always looking forward to the newest technological advancement. Although they've been friends for a longer period, their love for tech brought them much closer and made them who they are today.

# Index

## A

Actions while on a call ..................... 93
Add Calendars .................................. 70
Advanced Wi-Fi settings .......... 15, 149
Alarm ............................................... 72
Always On Display .......... 16, 17, 18, 22
Answer a call .................................... 92
AOD clock style ................................ 17
App Icons ......................................... 27
AR Zone ........................................... 66

## B

Block a number ................................ 95
Bookmarks ....................................... 84
Browser Tabs ................................... 84

## C

Calendar Alert Styles ....................... 71
Call log ............................................ 95

Call or Message a Contact ............... 78
Call pop-up settings ......................... 94
Connecting to a VPN ..................... 162
Create a movie .............................. 133
Create an Event ............................... 71
Create notes .................................... 46
Customize the Home Screen ........... 27

## D

Decline a call ................................... 92
Delete call records .......................... 95
Delete contacts .......................... 83, 92
Deleting a folder ............................. 60

## E

Edit a Contact .................................. 78
Edit notes ...................................... 100
Edit pictures .................................. 129
Edit videos .................................... 131
Emergency Alerts ............................ 87
End a call ........................................ 93

eSIM ................................................... 4
Export contacts ............................... 82

**F**

Face Recognition ............................ 19

**G**

Groups .............................................. 79

**H**

Hide apps .......................................... 33
Home screen settings ..................... 31
How to Create and Use Folders ....... 28

**I**

Import contacts .............................. 82
Internet Settings ............................. 86

**L**

Link contacts ................................... 82
Live Focus ...................................... 120

**M**

Making a call with Speed dial .......... 97
Making a Phone call ........................ 91
Manage calls ................................... 94
Managing a VPN ............................ 161
Managing Face Recognition ............ 19

Manually connect to a Wi-Fi network
.................................................. 148
Message Settings ........................... 88
Moving folder to my home screen .. 59

**N**

Notification Panel .......................... 35

**O**

Open a Bookmark .......................... 84

**P**

Password 12, 13, 14, 15, 16, 18, 19, 21, 23, 157, 158
Pattern ... 12, 13, 15, 16, 18, 19, 21, 23
Phone settings ................................ 97
Pictures ......................................... 122
PIN .......... 12, 13, 15, 16, 18, 19, 21, 23
Place a multiparty call .................... 98
power off menu ....................... 26, 35

**Q**

Quick settings ................................. 36

**R**

Recording Videos .......................... 120
recovery mode ............................... 26
Removing Speed dial number ......... 97

Rotate to landscape mode.............. 33

## S

Samsung Smart Switch...................... 8
Save a Web Page............................ 84
Saving a number from recent calls . 95
Scene Optimizer........................... 120
Screen Lock .................................... 12
Screenshot .................................... 134
Secret Mode ................................... 85
Send SOS Messages ........................ 87
Share a Contact.............................. 79
Share pictures and videos............ 132
Show battery percentage ............... 34
Show music information ................ 17
Smart Lock ..................................... 15
Smart Switch ....................8, 9, 10, 11
Speed dials..................................... 96
Status Bar....................................... 33
Stopwatch...................................... 75

## T

Themes .......................................... 29
Time Zone Converter ..................... 74
Timer.............................................. 75
Turn on Data Saver ...................... 155

## U

Unlink contacts ...............................82
Unpair from a Bluetooth Device....152
USB-OTG adapter .............................9
Use Palm Swipe to Capture a
 Screenshot ...............................134
Using Fingerprint ............................21
Using swipes to call ........................91

## V

Video calls......................................98
Video enhancer ............................131
View pictures................................128
View videos ..................................130
Voicemail........................................97

## W

Wallpaper .......................................28
Weather Settings............................75
When S Pen is removed..................54
Widget ...........................................30
Wi-Fi calling ...................................99
Wi-Fi Direct..................................150
Wi-Fi Sharing ...............................159
World clock....................................73

Made in the USA
Monee, IL
02 July 2021